Dear Stuart:

Charles has read this book that I wrote and he really wants others to do the same thing. I really hope that my book speaks to you in a meaningful way and that you also enjoy it!

Thank you very much,

Lisa

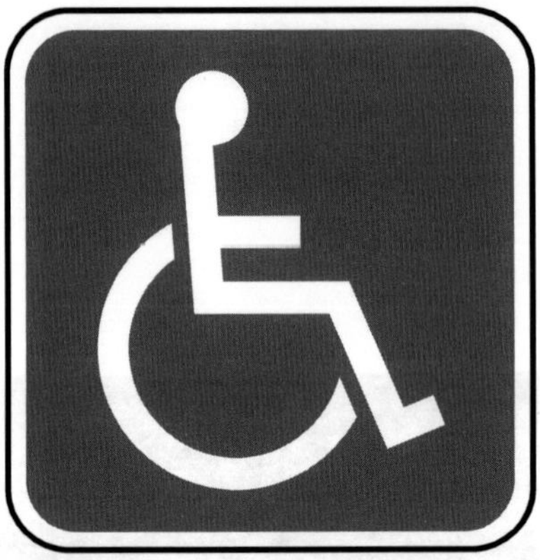

WHAT MY WHEELCHAIR TAUGHT ME

— one woman's journey —

Lisa Dianne Jones

◆ FriesenPress

Suite 300 - 990 Fort St
Victoria, BC, V8V 3K2
Canada

www.friesenpress.com

Copyright © 2020 by Lisa Dianne Jones
First Edition — 2019

All rights reserved.

No part of this publication may be reproduced in any form, or by any means, electronic or mechanical, including photocopying, recording, or any information browsing, storage, or retrieval system, without permission in writing from FriesenPress.

ISBN
978-1-5255-5384-4 (Hardcover)
978-1-5255-5385-1 (Paperback)
978-1-5255-5386-8 (eBook)

1. BIOGRAPHY & AUTOBIOGRAPHY, PEOPLE WITH DISABILITIES

Distributed to the trade by The Ingram Book Company

DEDICATION

To the delightfully strong Jones women, young and old,
and to my amazing friends and family who sustained me
while I wrote this book.

REVIEWS

This book is a treasure for anyone wanting to understand life with a disability, or wanting to explore human nature in any form. It is a song of praise to kindness, stubbornness and interdependence, sung through the voice of a woman who was written off more than once in life. A great and moving read!

John Butler

In reading this enjoyable book I discovered a courageous, determined woman who sought only what we all seek, to live a life of self-determination and optimized potential. Despite many obstacles she shows us how she does this so capably. Among these is her ability to fully occupy the events and moments of her life with awareness and focused attention. Her message to all, whether they identify a disability or not, is how to live life with presence, ingenuity, patience and so much Love.

Nancy Milne

Fantastic Book! Lisa's examination of her own life will cause you to examine yours.

Mathew Kirby

Inspiring, powerful, and painstakingly authentic. What we live through pales in comparison to the obstacles and challenges Lisa has to endure. Her courage and tenacity conquer them all. Lisa's cup is always half-full. No, it is filled to the brim.

Stella Ng

TABLE OF CONTENTS

Foreword	11
Dear Reader....	12
My Paradox: Normal or Not?	13
My Parents	15
The Jones Kids	17
Me	17
Steve	18
Us	19
Life Moments with My Grandparents, My Aunt, and My Uncle	23
Treatment Centre Years	31
School and the Primacy of Washrooms	36
I Refuse. I Become.	45
The Me People See	47
Reversal	52
University Experiences	56
Wanting Children	64
Early Years as a Mother	73
Beyond My Own Motherhood	81
My Best Volunteer Experiences	84
My Amazing Human Connections	89
My People of Faith	89
A Friend, a Family, a Tree	91
From Childhood to Forever	93
My Working Sisters	94
Newcomers Become Friends	96
Helpers Who Became Friends	97
The Godfather	97

    My Four Musketeers   97
    My Friend, My Cabbie   98
    A Friend Who Makes Beautiful Things   99
    The Man I Love   100
    Thoughts on Friendship   102

My House, Our Home   104
My Rant   109
That Was Then and This is Now   113
What I've Learned and Messages I Want to Share   118
Final Words from Friends   123
About the Author   127

FOREWORD

I know a strong woman. You might envision a great world leader or a powerful businesswoman, a famous surgeon or a humble, devout servant of the poor.

The strong woman I know is Lisa Jones. She's unlike any other woman I have known. She is a warrior, a perseverant advocate, a kind and gentle soul, and the passionate lover of her daughters and her partner.

In my profession, I am used to serving, advocating, and teaching. But I haven't needed to teach Lisa anything. She is the one who teaches me. She has taught me how physical challenges impact on every minute of an affected person's life, but she has also taught me that a strong, loving, optimistic and alive spirit can make a person soar over those challenges and positively impact on the lives of so many.

She is a super hero.

Dr. Lori Coman-Wood

DEAR READER....

I'm very happy right now.

First, I'm happy because this book is done. Long ago I sensed that I should write this book, but when I got started on the process I wasn't at all sure I could write it. Would my memories and observations be enough for a book? Did I have the skills to wrap the right words around those memories and observations? Would anyone want to read it?

Soon it occurred to me that writing the book would be like eating an elephant: one bite at a time, one word at a time. Trying to gulp down an elephant in one sitting is a pretty good way to get severe indigestion (especially for a vegetarian like me). I started writing in small bites and it became easier and easier to write a little more at each sitting. As a result, my book is finally here.

Secondly, I'm happy because you're reading this introduction. Maybe it means you're interested and you'll read more of this book. I hope you do. I hope that something you read in the book gives you an insight, an idea, hope, courage, confidence, and the desire to live your life as authentically as you need to. That's my wish for you, dear reader. Enjoy it!

MY PARADOX: NORMAL OR NOT?

There is a paradox at the heart of this book because there is a paradox at the core of my life, a paradox I share with just about everybody who has a disability.

On one hand, I sometimes dream about being like everybody else. I strive to be like everybody else, I go to great pains to point out, quite rightly, that my similarities to other people outweigh my differences from other people.

On the other hand, I am not like everybody else. I can't do some things that other people do, even though I develop workarounds that compensate for what I can't do. Just because of my wheelchair I sometimes look and act differently than other people do. Society marks me as a different creature because of it.

So is this book about Lisa Jones, the soulmate to everyone else, and about how I lead a normal life? Or is it about Lisa Jones the woman with a disability, and how my life is shaped by that disability and the world's reaction to it?

The book is about both, but it focuses more on Lisa Jones, the woman with a disability, so I can talk about the effects a disability has had on my life.

If you are a reader who doesn't have a significant disability, you might want to know how my disability affects my life. But if you are a reader with a significant disability, you might find it comforting to read about a kindred spirit striving, as you do, to live a normal life when you are different.

While I call my reminiscences "What My Wheelchair Taught Me", it's fair to say that my wheelchair isn't actually a teacher. It's an integrated hunk of metal, plastic, and rubber that gets me from place to place and lets me sit in relative comfort, no matter where I am. I'm not "confined" to the wheelchair: I'm liberated by it.

Yet it's more than a collection of hardware. When people meet me they inevitably see the wheelchair in the front of their minds. They often judge me based not on who I am, but on the collection of hardware on which I sit. So the wheelchair assumes symbolic importance, like a third person in the room and in my life—an occasionally annoying friend to me, but a friend nonetheless. The three-way interaction among me, the wheelchair, and the world, mediated by symbols, actually does the teaching.

I use the word "wheelchair" in the singular, but I've had a succession of wheelchairs over the years, ranging from a simple little wooden chair built by my father when I first went to school, to a contemporary electric wheelchair. And at any one time I have two chairs—a chair without a motor that I or my friends can manually propel (light enough to be folded and put in a car trunk) and an electric chair that seems heavy as a tank but that can move me at the same speed as a fast walk. In fact, when I'm on what are supposed to be leisurely strolls with walking friends, they sometimes complain that I move too fast for them to keep up with me.

But no matter what wheelchair I've used, it has liberated me by giving me mobility. It has also imprisoned me in the web of other people's assumptions about what the person in the chair can do and cannot do.

MY PARENTS

*Two lovely parents =
one loving daughter*

To know who I was and who I am, you should learn a bit about the wonderful people who first surrounded me, and surround me still.

My parents are strong and loving people. My dad has always been a caring, detail oriented man. My mom has always been a woman with a huge caring heart. They shaped my personality.

They were typical parents of the 60s and 70s. My father worked every day and I saw him mostly in the evening. My mom was a stay at home mother until I was about 12 years old.

In 1953 at the age of twenty-two my father emigrated from his parental home in West Drayton, a western suburb of London England, because he objected to being drafted into the British army. As a result of his English school credentials he acquired two jobs in Canada that used and developed his engineering and draftsmanship skills. In his first job, in Cobourg Ontario, he designed and developed ejection seats for the

Avro Canada CF-105 Arrow, the most advanced military fighter plane ever developed by the Canadian aviation industry. However, in February 1959 the Canadian government scuttled development of the Arrow and destroyed all plans and prototypes of the plane. The cancellation caused considerable political controversy at the time.

To find new work, Dad responded to a job posting to help design nuclear reactors in Chalk River Ontario for Atomic Energy of Canada Limited (AECL), an organization created by the government in 1952 to supply nuclear energy for medical and scientific applications.

Chalk River, on the Ottawa River, was not the main residential site for AECL workers. An entirely new town—Deep River—had been created in the 50s, ten kilometers east of Chalk River, to serve that purpose.

Once he landed the job, Dad went to Deep River to find a place to live and to open a bank account at the Bank of Montreal, the only bank branch in the area. Mom worked there as a teller, saving her earnings to pay for training as a registered nurse at the Ottawa Hospital. She shelved that dream when she met my dad. She was smitten by his looks and his English accent. Dad was smitten by her beauty and her personality. I must say (biased as I am) that she is still beautiful: my mom and my two daughters remain the most beautiful women I've ever known.

Mom had just turned nineteen when she married my dad, who was then twenty-five.

Early in their married life they enjoyed boating and curling. My dad, the eternal handyman, helped Mom's parents build their house in Deep River.

Much as Mom loved Dad's English accent, it puzzled her at times. She told me he once said to her, "I need to go to the hardware store to buy faucets." She asked him: "Four sets of what?"

THE JONES KIDS

Me

Creating a family was an unexpected and painful struggle for them.

Their first child, a boy, lived for 48 hours. I was their second child. Their third child, a girl, lived for less than 24 hours. My mother later miscarried twins.

I was born three months prematurely, weighing only three pounds and five ounces, on a January day in 1962 at Deep River's small hospital. It was a facility with little experience meeting the needs of premature babies. I spent the first months of my life in an incubator, but hospital staff in the sixties were unaware of the need to maintain a consistent oxygen flow for babies in incubators. When I turned blue from lack of oxygen, the oxygen in the incubator was switched on but once I returned to a proper pink color the oxygen was switched off. I don't know whether my premature birth or the early incubator care I received caused me to have cerebral palsy—a condition that often stems from damage to a fetal or newborn's brain when that brain is deprived of oxygen, even for a few minutes. Parts of the brain that control muscle coordination can be damaged, and sometimes the little one's thinking capacities are damaged too.

It wasn't immediately apparent to my parents that I was a baby with challenges. But after a few months they saw I wasn't progressing physically the way other babies would. I would wiggle away like other babies, but I couldn't crawl or sit up unassisted.

When my parents pointed out my difficulties to our family doctor, he diagnosed my problems as the result of cerebral palsy.

Despite the diagnosis, my parents didn't know what kind of kid they had on their hands. Would I ever walk? Would my ability to speak clearly be affected? Would my intellectual capacity be hampered?

In the 1960's and earlier, doctors often recommended to vulnerable and fearful parents that their children with major physical or mental health challenges should be institutionalized. My mom and dad were advised by health care professionals that it would be hard for them to raise me and that an institution where I could be cared for with others of my kind would be best.

But the same raw courage that led my parents to keep trying to have a child after their first child perished was the same courage that led them to reject that advice. I was stuck with them, they were stuck with me. I have been ever grateful for the choice they made.

Steve

My brother and I sharing a cookie. I control the cookie.

Two years after I was born, Mom and Dad took me to a strange building where we picked up a slightly chubby little boy. They told me he was my brother and that his name was Steven. He was cute and I was happy to have a brother. I remember (at just two years old) that a lady in the building said to me, "I have something very important for you to do. You need to hold on to this bottle and give it to your brother." I gave it to him as soon as we were in the car.

My mom quickly found out that my brother was too chubby because his foster mother had been giving him pureed baby food that shouldn't be given to babies until they are six to eight months old. He also desperately needed a good wash. She and one of our neighbors bathed him as soon as we got home. Mom put him back on a milk diet.

Us

When I was three years old we moved from Deep River to Erindale Woodlands, a burgeoning archetypical suburban community west of Toronto. Erindale Woodlands was absorbed into the Town (later City) of Mississauga in 1968.

My dad had been told that he would get a promotion and a raise if he joined the Sheridan Park branch of Atomic Energy of Canada, located ten minutes away from our new house. In addition, my parents had learned that from Erindale Woodlands they would be able to take me fairly easily (in those days before highway gridlock) to and from the Ontario Crippled Children's Centre in Toronto, where I could learn to walk.

Our house—the house where my parents still live—was a bungalow on a lovely street that curved like a racetrack around an elongated central grass boulevard. Both my parents have a passion for neatness and order (a passion I share), and our suburban yard gave my dad a chance to build flowerbeds, manicure a lawn front and back, and, when I was ten, install a swimming pool. It also gave my mother a chance to decorate a home with understated elegance. Since the house was a bungalow I didn't face the challenge of getting to a second floor, but it had no special accessibility features inside the house and no ramps to get from the front or back door to the ground level outside. But everything I needed was on the main floor. I crawled from place to place to get where I needed to be. Crawling was my main mode of mobility until I started school, although I also learned to stand for brief periods and maneuver a few feet clinging to furniture, even though it wasn't my preferred way of getting around—it was too slow for a dedicated, intent, and highly competent crawler. Mom or Dad would lift me onto the couch, chairs, the toilet, or my bed and would carry me places when we went outside. I also crawled around in the back yard and I could often be found in my best girlfriend's next-door back yard. She was one grade ahead of me in school, but we became inseparable friends from the time I was in grade one until we both left home to go to university. She never seemed to care that I crawled or later used a wheelchair.

As we grew up, she and I swam almost every summer day in the in-ground pool Dad had installed. She became adept at jumping over the fence that separated our two back yards, but she ripped her jeans several times during these daily fence jumps. We spent hours in the water over hot lazy summers that seemed to go on forever. Moving around in water was easier for me than maneuvering across a grassy lawn—I loved the added freedom that water gave me as long as I wasn't far from an edge to cling to if I got into trouble. Around the time our pool was installed I started having lunch at her house on school days because my mom was studying to become a registered nursing assistant (RNA). Mom graduated from the program and took a job as an RNA at the Mississauga Hospital—a job she loved because it appealed to her natural talents and it nurtured the happiness she felt when helping people. She worked there for two years until a back injury forced her to leave the work. I was proud of Mom the Nurse, but over the decades I've been even prouder of the help she has given, time after time, to people around her.

As a young child I was far from immobile. I was adventurous. I thought nothing of sitting on the floor, putting my legs over each stair and sliding myself down on my bottom, stair by stair, to the basement while my little brother walked down the stairs protectively beside me. We did this so we could watch cartoons in the basement TV room really early on weekend mornings, sharing a box of cheerios with each other before Mom and Dad woke up.

As I got older and regularly used a wheelchair I learned how to function as best as I could in a non-accessible environment, using whatever was at hand. For example, the bathroom sink vanity became the thing that I leaned on when I needed to get out of my chair and onto the toilet. Several times I tore the towel rack off the bathroom wall because I used it as a grab bar: it was a good thing Dad knew how to repair things.

I was happy there.

In addition to my close relationship with my brother, I developed connections and friendships with many other kids on our street. I wasn't at all shy about making the first move to meet them. They got used to seeing me crawl over to them, and I did my best to keep up with them as they ran.

I often sat on the front porch or the front lawn absorbing the world as it went by. The art of "front porching" and smiling or waving at passersby became a lifelong habit, a way of engaging others, the first step in striking up conversations and starting friendships, and helping folks to find out that I'm not scary after all.

My friends often sat down on the porch or the grass with me and we played. I raised myself up on my knees when I needed to reach something or to turn a skipping rope for my friends.

My brother and I were very close. Like most children, we showed our closeness by what we did together. We both loved to watch TV, and we did a lot of coloring and crafts.

We grew up knowing that strict compliance to our parents' rules was expected, and that if we didn't comply, some sort of punishment would result. Fortunately both of us grew up adhering to the rules most of the time. My dad has always taken great pride in an orderly and clean house, and he didn't easily tolerate his kids making a mess: Steve and I knew that we had to keep things tidy. We weren't allowed to stick anything on the walls—the most challenging rule for both of us. As a young teen I wanted to hang a poster of Shaun Cassidy—the heartthrob of that time—on my bedroom wall. It never happened.

Sunday was a favorite day for my brother and me when we were young—not only because there was no school or homework to deal with in the evening on Sunday, but also because the family had our Sunday dinners on TV tables in our basement. Dad sometimes lit a fire in the basement's stone fireplace and let us roast marshmallows on sticks over the flames. As well, our Sunday dinners were the best of the week. We often had roast beef and mashed potatoes with gravy and peas. My mom, being a stay-at-home mom then, always made us a pie or a cake for that day. We were also allowed to watch *Mutual of Omaha's Wild Kingdom* and *The Wonderful World of Disney* while we were eating.

Friday nights were special too. When Steve and I were young, Mom took a part-time job as a teller at the Bank of Montreal. She worked on Friday nights and would be home by 8:00 p.m. This was another night when we were allowed to watch TV, so Steven and I would lie on his bed watching *Dallas* and *The Rockford Files*. Without fail, Mom brought home treats for us on Friday night after her work. We each got a bag of chips, a chocolate bar, and a can of pop. We felt we were being overindulged but we ate everything by the time we went to bed.

Despite my disability my parents didn't bubble-wrap me. They both tried hard to make sure I had a pretty normal childhood. Apart from the restrictions that my intensive physiotherapy imposed, I was still expected to do well in school.

On occasions my brother and I had one-on-one time with our mom and dad. My favorite times with Mom have been our shopping trips. She has a huge heart and she would think nothing about finding something that I liked and buying it for me. "Oh, I'll buy that for you" is a phrase I heard very often from her. I hear it from her even now that I have children of my own. When she and I are in a mall, we still stop at a food court or a restaurant to enjoy a meal, a coffee, or a treat together and discuss what's on our minds. She is also generous to her friends. At the age of eighty she still regularly drove one of her friends to cancer treatments. It was rarer for Dad and me to go out somewhere, but he routinely took my brother to hockey and soccer practices and games.

One of my fondest memories is a "date" I had with Dad when I was twelve. Dad enjoys country music, so he and I went to see *Coal Miner's Daughter*, a movie about country music superstar Loretta Lynn. I remember how special I felt sharing a large drink of pop and a box of popcorn with a man who was holding my hand and singing along with the songs in the movie. He made me feel proud to be his daughter.

My parents taught me not to expect anything less of myself because of my disability. I remember saying to Dad when I was fourteen, "I need some money." His response: "OK, get a job." So I did. A classmate told me about a nearby day care center that wanted to pay someone to stay with the children in the late afternoon and early evening until late-arriving parents picked up their kids, and then record parent arrival times and how often parents were late picking up their kids. I got the job.

Because Mom and Dad didn't lower their expectations of me, I developed a MacGyver approach to life. MacGyver was the resourceful secret agent on the 80s TV show of the same name who could solve any problem with spit, a toilet paper roll, three paper clips, and a shoelace. Great stuff! He never lost his cool. Maybe he knew he could always find some kind of innovative solution to foil the bad guys. I loved that. Over time I realized that, like MacGyver, I've always found a tool or method I can use in some way in any situation.

By using unconventional problem-solving skills I became as independent as possible, I found ways to do difficult things and to meet the needs of my children and other people important in my life. I have lived the phrase "Where there is a will, there is a way".

My mom and dad live by the same motto too. So do my magnificently resourceful daughters.

Soon after we moved to Erindale Woodlands, Dad joined the Erindale-Mississauga Lions Club to connect with other men. The Lions is a service club whose mission includes bettering the quality of life for people with disabilities.

In 1971 a group of parents in Mississauga decided that children with disabilities in Peel and Halton needed a rehabilitation center. They formed the Credit Valley Association for Handicapped Children (CVAHC), elected a board of directors and obtained a charter. Dad heard about this initiative and it excited him. He hoped the center would be built soon enough for me to benefit from it, so Mom wouldn't need to drive me to and from Toronto for my every two week therapy check-in appointments. Dad persuaded his Lions Club members to get involved in this project. They led a fundraising drive, making it possible for Credit Valley Treatment Centre for Children to open in 1978. By then my own connection with the Ontario Crippled Children's Centre had ended and I was considered too old to be a client of the Credit Valley Centre (now known as Erinoak Centre for Treatment and Development).

I've always been proud of my dad for being a leader, for taking the initiative and mobilizing others to help create the Centre. I had my own difficult time in a treatment center, but the Credit Valley Centre was a brighter place with no live-in requirements and it made a greater effort to find out what works best for children and their families. It continues to enrich the lives of many young people with disabilities.

LIFE MOMENTS WITH MY GRANDPARENTS, MY AUNT, AND MY UNCLE

My mom's parents lived in Deep River. My dad's parents lived in West Drayton in the County of Middlesex England, a western suburb of Greater London.

Mom's parents were the relatives that my brother and I saw the most when we were children, because we lived closer to them—although they were a seven hour drive away when we moved from Deep River to Mississauga.

My Canadian grandma had Finnish roots. She easily spoke both Finnish and English. She was not a tall woman. She had light brown hair and gorgeous deep blue eyes. Make-up, jewelry, and clean matching clothes were very important to my grandma. She was also adept at laundry and ironing. She ironed everything, including underwear.

Much of her life was shaped by the Great Depression of the 1930s: she was just sixteen in 1930. During the Depression many people couldn't be certain about the stability of their futures, so they made consistency and order vital components of their everyday lives. Grandma made consistency and order her priorities forever. My mom told me that Grandma gave her kids a pre-planned meal every night of the week: Wednesday's supper was always spaghetti night, Friday was always fish night.

Although Grandma never worked full-time, in the latter part of her life she was a nursery school teacher and a male choir instructor, and she played the piano for a dance class.

Whenever we went to visit Grandma (unless it was a holiday evening when we arrived), she changed her rigid meal schedule enough to make us a dinner of spaghetti and a green salad. There were also always two tins of slightly burnt homemade cookies (oatmeal and chocolate chip) in the bottom drawer in her kitchen perhaps purposely put there so I could easily crawl over to the drawer and get them out. On top of her china cabinet in the dining room you could also always find a small glass dish of scotch mint candies. My brother, my cousins, and I used to grab the mints and eat them as often as we could. My brother and cousins could reach them so I just became a grateful recipient. Whenever they got one, so did I! Grandma herself loved chocolate. When there was no other form of chocolate around, you could sometimes see her eating up the chocolate chips that she had intended for her next batch of cookies.

Grandma was impressed by the voracious reader that I became as a young girl. In the back yard of their house there was an old-fashioned wooden patio swing with cushions on the seat, an arm rest at each end, and a fabric canopy cover on top. It was wide enough to comfortably seat three adults. On a hot summer day I liked nothing better than lounging on the wide comfortable seat as long as possible, reading comics and library books. If I was alone on it I could lie down for a little snooze if I wanted. Sometimes I called out to Grandma for a sandwich, some cookies or a drink. She always brought me something.

I felt comfortable and safe in that house. It smelled woodsy, with a tang of salt water despite its distance from any ocean.

I once asked my mom, "Why are Grandma's bed sheets so stiff?" She said it was because Grandma always hung them outside to dry so they don't get soft as they do when dried in the dryer. Grandma liked to save money that way.

Grandma used a pressure cooker to cook tough cuts of meat. This contraption scared the heck out of me. Sometimes it scared her too.

The old-fashioned version of this device produced steam, which cooked food faster by raising the boiling point. Grandma's cooker had a jiggle top that sat on the steam vent on the lid. As steam rose through it, the jiggle top wiggled rhythmically and very loudly. To a little girl it looked like the plume of steam would hit the ceiling and damage it. At a crucial moment Grandma had to reduce the heat on the stove to reduce the steaming process, but that never happened before I was convinced that something dangerous and explosive was about to occur. I later learned that a cook should remove food from the pot shortly after the steaming process ended or the meat took on the consistency of lumpy baby food. Unfortunately for those who ate her handiwork, Grandma didn't always remember that.

Once when my brother and I were quite young, Mom and Dad went on a week's vacation and Grandma looked after my brother and me. She must have felt generous that week because she took the two of us to a toy store. She bought my brother a yellow metal toy Tonka dump truck and she bought me a beautiful glass tea set so I could have a tea party with my favorite doll Kimberly. Grandma had given me that doll for Christmas. My brother and I happily played outside, he in the sand and I on the grass. I was having trouble getting my tea party dishes to stay upright on the grass. I noticed a nearby garbage pail that had a lid. I grabbed the pail, put the lid on top and put the tea party dishes on the lid. The garbage pail had become my elegant tea-table.

In a short while it started to rain. Grandma told us to come in. She wasn't too happy with me the next day, after she heard the garbage truck and realized that my pretty glass tea set was now gone. Because the pieces were on top of the garbage pail the garbage man simply assumed that everything in or on top of the pail was garbage.

During some of our visits with my grandparents, my Mom's younger brother would be there too. Sometimes he took Steve, the other grandkids, and me to Laurentian View Dairy. In my little girl opinion they had the biggest and best strawberry ice cream cones on the planet. I was always ready and willing to go there.

My uncle had an uncanny ability to find quarters and dimes hidden in his nieces and nephews, which he was always willing to give to us. "What's that money doing in your ear?" he would say, then reach up close to the ear and pull out a coin. It took us years to figure out that he had the money hidden in his hand. The luxury of possessing a huge strawberry ice cream cone, and some change in our hands at the same moment, made all of us kids feel very special. In my childhood you could buy penny candies in corner stores and carry the sweet cargo away in a small brown paper bag, so even having just a nickel or a dime meant you could go to a candy store and choose your treat. My favorite was Double Bubble bubble gum. It came with a comic strip inside the wrapper and a piece of beautiful pink (but hard as a rock) bubble gum. It took me a while to learn how to blow bubbles with that stuff, but I loved doing it.

Mom's younger sister, my aunt, was also good to all the grandchildren. She was very good at sewing and knitting: her daughter (my cousin) and I were recipients of cute homemade dresses, and pink and yellow knitted sweaters. Years later when I lived in residence at Carleton University in Ottawa, I lived close enough to my aunt and cousins to visit them regularly. I was often invited to their house for a weekend dinner. These visits made my relationship with my aunt even closer.

My maternal grandfather was a very quiet Scottish man. He had been trained as a machinist and tool maker in Dundee Scotland. He had a full head of white hair (shaved short by Grandma) and green eyes. He would let me sit on his lap so we could watch *Bugs Bunny* and other cartoons together on their television.

Early in his working life Grandpa moved the family from Timmins to Deep River because he hoped to get a job at the Canadian Nuclear Laboratories in nearby Chalk River. Grandpa was quickly hired by them because his skills as a machinist were essential in helping to create Canada's nuclear energy industry. He also used his knowledge to help repair things for the Town of Deep River and the Laurentian View Dairy.

Because we visited most often during statutory holiday weekends when he wasn't at work, I most often remember him sitting in his rocking chair in the living room reading newspapers and smoking cigarettes. During our winter visits I sometimes heard the back doorbell of the house ringing: it was people calling on him to sharpen their skates, a small seasonal side job that Grandpa, always a good Scottish opportunist, took on. Whatever noisy equipment Grandpa had in the basement, it obviously resulted in many people having sharp skates.

Grandpa was not picky about his meals. In the morning when I was at his house, I watched him simply take whatever meat was left over in the fridge and turn it into a sandwich that would sustain him before he went outside to tend to the garden, cut the grass, or shovel snow. I thought it was funny that he was allowed to have a sandwich for breakfast. One time he encouraged me to eat some typically Scottish porridge he had made with salty water. The resulting product was, to the eyes and palate of a child, a gluey grey horrible mess. Grandma understood my discontent and gave me some of the ancient stale cheerios cereal that she kept in the cupboard above the stove. Despite their stale taste, the cheerios were much better than salt-laced porridge.

Grandpa was always happy when we had holiday dinners together because it meant we could have at least two kinds of pie. When asked which one he wanted, he would always say: "Give me a smidge of both. I need to find out if they are any good." Using that strategy, the man made sure he could guiltlessly enjoy multiple desserts. As his response to the dessert question became predictable, all his grandchildren would giggle as soon as Grandma asked him what kind of pie he wanted.

When my mom's father retired, my grandparents became Florida snow birds. This gave my brother and me the opportunity to visit them in Tampa Bay with Mom and Dad a few times during our junior high school March Break vacations.

Our first visit took place when I was in seventh grade. I remember the drive from the airport to my grandparents' trailer was perfumed with the smell of orange blossoms. Mom told me they were Florida's official state flower. I also got my first look at a real palm tree—much more robust than occasional out-of-place shrunken plastic palm trees in Mississauga's shopping malls. I was impressed by how much more majestic and summery the palm tree seemed compared to our boring Canadian birches and pines.

The original mobile home owned by my grandparents was an old school bus that had been converted to a simple and very crowded house trailer. There was enough room for all six of us to sleep, but room for anything else was very limited. I learned that cramped space is always more bearable when you share it with people you love.

When the weather was good we ate all our meals outside. Almost everything was barbecued. We took showers in public washrooms that were part of the campground.

All of this worked well except once, when it rained continuously for four days in a row. Being stuck inside watching soap operas, game shows, and the news on a tiny TV was no one's concept of a fun vacation. But once the sun came back out, the world changed for us all. Then, you could go outside wearing just a bathing suit or a simple top and shorts. I was delighted to be shoeless. I loved the warm feel of the sun all over me.

This first winter vacation in a warm place confirmed to me and to those around me that I will always be a warmth lover. Part of my sun worship stems from the susceptibility to cold that some people using wheelchairs may also experience. Since we can't warm our bodies by vigorous walking, we rely on external heat to keep us warm. I'm a lover of sweaters, shawls, ponchos, lovely bulky knitted socks—but most of all I love the sun, even when those around me are damp sponges during summer heat waves (I commiserate with them as they struggle to live with their disability).

The simplicity of life in Florida during a vacation was what my brother and I enjoyed the most. There was a swimming pool at the campground, and Clearwater Beach was a short car ride away. Sitting on the beach with a cool drink and the chance to gorge on french fries or an ice cream cone from a nearby food truck satisfied me for many hours. Whenever we went to Florida we made it to the beach every day that the weather allowed. My family members helped me get in and out of the water from time to time. Mom and Dad taught me to swim in our backyard pool and I felt comfortable alone in a pool, knowing I could grab hold of the pool side if I was tired, but I have always felt uncomfortable in a large uncontained water-filled space. On a beach I was content to sit in a lawn chair and watch other people swim and build sand castles. I also loved to just chat with my grandparents, especially when they didn't have to deal with the demands of an up-north holiday gathering like Christmas. Grandma always asked me about school and told me she was proud of my achievements.

Near the beach there were a number of little shops. Most people that went into them came out wearing a brand new bathing suit. I loved the bright, light, cheerful clothing in the shops, happy that for a while I didn't need my own dull boreal companions—a jacket or thick sweater—to keep warm.

Evenings during these visits involved board games like Scrabble and a few marshmallows roasted over the barbeque before we all snugged ourselves back into the bus trailer and went off to sleep, dreaming of hot sun and the warmth of family.

Other visits to my grandparents in Florida were just as pleasant but I will always remember the first visit, with its deluge of new smells, sights, sounds, and people, as the most beautiful visit.

I first met my dad's parents at the age of six when they first visited Canada. They returned to Canada to see us when I was eleven. When I graduated from high school in 1980, Mom, Dad, my brother, and I flew to England and visited my grandparents in their house in the London suburb of West Drayton.

During their first stay in Canada with us, I was impressed that my grandfather always seemed to wear a suit and a tie. It made him look very important and handsome, and as a little girl I thought, wow, he must still go to work a lot! I learned that he had been a railroad engineer with the Great Western Railway.

My grandmother's background was Swiss. She was quieter than my grandfather and she always wore dresses. She reminded me of the Queen because she wore pretty hats with what she termed her neat and proper clothing. I look a bit like her. She had brown eyes and slightly curly brown-grey hair. She influenced my love for reading because she enjoyed reading stories and playing board games like checkers with my brother and me. To Grandma that game was called draughts. Before she married my grandfather, she had worked for the Gramophone Company (later renamed EMI Records). Her job was to listen to vinyl records that came off the press to ensure they sounded right and played properly. After that, she worked as a school lunch lady for children whose parents served in the Second World War. At any time, anyone serving in the war could also come into the school for a free meal.

During my grandparents' visits I learned some of the words that English people use to describe items they use and the clothing they wear—words that were strange but fascinating to a Canadian girl:

> The boot is the word used in England for the trunk of a car.
>
> A layette is a collection of clothes, blankets, booties, and hats for newborns.
>
> A jumper is a sweater and a vest is an undershirt.
>
> Knickers is the word used in England for underwear.
>
> Diapers are known as nappies, a pinny (short for pinafore) is an apron, and a Macintosh is a raincoat.
>
> Chips are french fries. Crisps are potato chips.

My grandpa once said to me, "Ducky, do you want to play naughts and crosses with me?" I had no clue what that meant. He explained to me that ducky is a term of endearment like "honey" and naughts and crosses means playing x's and o's, a game I always won when I played against Grandpa—but maybe, being Grandpa, he let me win.

Grandpa was also very affectionate towards me, fond of showing his affection by handing me sweets (candies). He was a cute-looking man with white hair, he was short and slender, and like Grandma he considered clean and proper clothing to be important. I was fascinated by his ability to smoke cigarettes while rarely removing the piece of ash that grew longer and longer as he held the cigarette securely on his bottom lip. It was impossible to avoid thinking that the ash would fall off and burn him. Sometimes if you looked carefully you could see little burn holes on his shirt or jumper, despite his pride in dressing properly.

Grandma was more reserved but she was interested in what my brother and I were doing in school and she often inquired. Her common phrase was "once around me, twice around a tire." That was her way of implying that she was chubbier than a tire when we tried to hug her, although I never saw her that way. I cared more about the love in the hug than the width of the hugger.

My grandparents' house in West Drayton was similar to townhouses in Canada, with a notable exception. When my family and I went to visit them in 1980 we were cold most of the time, even inside the house, because my grandparents didn't have central heating. That explained to my brother and me why there were so many blankets on the beds. While we slept we were toasty, but in the morning we wanted to do our washroom work as quickly as possible (the toilet was located in a room completely separate from the tub, shower, and sink) so we could get downstairs to bask in front of the living room's fireplace. Being cold, along with experiencing jet lag, meant that for the first few days of our ten day visit my family and I often just fell asleep on the couch near the fire. Eventually Mom took my brother and me to a store where she bought us wool sweaters. We kept those on every day until we came home.

It's not totally clear to me what kind of relationship my parents had with their parents. Dad has told me often that when he was young, "children were to be seen but not heard." In 1998, when he was recovering from non-Hodgkin's lymphoma, he told me that he was never taught or encouraged to show or express his feelings or emotions. Thankfully, he felt safe enough to do that when he was recovering from the cancer.

I think that both my mom and dad were raised in homes where strict unquestioning compliance to parental requests was expected. My brother and I grew up experiencing the same expectation from our parents. I believe that my parents were loved by their own parents, but I think they grew up in an era when the love of a parent for a child was implied rather than expressed. Happily, my parents expressed their love to my brother and me in words every day, and we received a ton of kisses. I try to be just as expressive to my own wonderful daughters.

None of these four loving grandparents, nor my aunt and uncle, ever conveyed any concern, worry or reservation about me being a little girl with a visible disability, nothing that caused me pain, anxiety or fear that they saw me as different and deficient. I was simply a cherished granddaughter and niece to people who were sometimes quiet by nature, but who were interesting, accepting and loving.

TREATMENT CENTRE YEARS

When I was between the ages of three and ten, my wheelchair taught me to be afraid. It also taught me about vulnerability, segregation, and incessant homesickness. During those years I spent time in a treatment facility—the Ontario Crippled Children's Centre on Rumsey Road in East York, part of Toronto.

Before those years, when we still lived in Deep River, a neighborhood friend of my mom who was a registered physiotherapist visited me periodically to help me become more mobile. Though I didn't have an official therapy routine with her, she visited our house from time to time to help me strengthen my muscles so I could experience my own independence. I was learning to stand myself up and take some steps.

Once we moved to Erindale Woodlands, the Ontario Crippled Children's Centre that I attended required that a strict protocol be followed to teach people how to walk. For that reason I was no longer allowed to perform the exercises I had learned from Mom's friend, as well exercises I had developed myself. There was no more taking steps either.

I became a part-time patient at the Crippled Children's Centre because society had decided that meaningful and valuable human beings were those who could walk. Since I couldn't walk, I needed to be fixed. Physiotherapists who worked in the Centre convinced my parents that intensive daily therapy provided at their facility could get me walking faster and better.

The Centre provided live-in service for children with disabilities. I resided there from Monday until Friday for about seven weeks each year when I was between the ages of three and ten. Some of us (including me) got to go home from Friday evening until Sunday evening.

There seemed to be a small number of nurses compared to the forty children who were in my ward.

This ward was comprised of five rooms on each side of a hallway. Four kids were in each room. Whenever I was a patient there, the room I was in always housed four girls. During my first stay the four of us in my room ranged in age from three, which was me, to about seven or eight years old. The rooms were nondescript—white walls, brown curtains, four hospital style beds with dark green bedspreads, four night stands, and one large washroom. From time to time birthday cards, Christmas cards or get-well cards were taped on the walls above our beds.

Some of us had flowers or a plant from our families on our nightstands. The nurses removed these from our rooms at night. They told us that because of a process called respiration, plants release oxygen during the day, but at night plants compete with people for oxygen and they release carbon dioxide, which is bad for humans. For that reason our plants and flowers were put in a separate room along with our wheelchairs, walkers, and crutches every night. On occasions when I had flowers, their removal each night angered me. I saw it as yet another thing the nurses did based on the belief that it would keep us safe, but that took away something that made us to feel special and loved.

Weekdays in the facility were regimented and based on a medical model. All of the kids ranging in age from about five to sixteen were wakened at 7:00 a.m. We weren't allowed to wear our own clothes (probably because the nurses didn't have the time or the energy to remember which clothes belonged to which person), so big carts filled with clothes arrived at the door of each four-person room every morning. After we were washed and dressed we were taken to a dining room. Breakfast was always a gluey porridge, which I never ate, toast and jam, and orange juice.

Our dining room was next to the ward for kids with cystic fibrosis. While we were trying to eat we heard nurses pounding on children's chests to release the mucus in their lungs, followed by coughing, gagging, and spitting.

After breakfast our temperatures were taken. If our patient charts revealed that any of us had not had a bowel movement in twenty-four hours, we became the lucky recipients of milk of magnesia or an enema. Enemas and other medical interventions were done on our beds with no curtains or privacy screens. We could all see everything that was being done to everyone else. We learned not to look.

Most of the rest of the day focused on intense physiotherapy. During our daily sessions we also endured the humiliation of being stripped to underwear only. Therapists then manipulated our bodies in multiple ways.

One of my weirdest treatments involved having ice cubes rubbed up and down my legs, followed by having my legs stroked by what looked like an electric paint brush and then having heat packs placed on the legs. This wasn't painful, but other procedures caused pain and buckets of tears among us.

When my first therapy session was over each day I was sent to a classroom of sorts. Because I was often the only patient who had attended a regular elementary school, the things I was taught in the Centre's classroom were at a lower level than my kindergarten class and even the grade two class I was in when I was released from the Centre for a second time and returned home.

There was rarely anything to be excited about in that environment, but one early evening in 1967 I was allowed to stay up until 8:30 to meet Eddie Shack. I had no idea who he was until an older patient explained that he was a famous Toronto Maple Leaf hockey player. This brush with celebrity was exciting to a five year old girl!

When each Friday came my spirits rose because I knew that I would go home for the weekend. The too few precious hours of a normal life with my family (and no inpatient therapy) were heaven to me. I could eat barbecued food. I could sit in a bubble bath in the morning for as long as I wanted. But I often cried on Saturday nights because I knew I had to go back to that place the next day.

Sitting in the back seat of Dad's car on a Sunday night for the hour-long drive back to the Centre, I would say desperate things to Mom and Dad: "Mom, please don't let Dad take me there. Can't we just go to get ice cream or a doughnut, please? Please Dad? I'll be good, I'll let you do my exercises, please let's go home!"

Those pleas were followed by a flood of tears. I wondered what I had done to make my parents want to send me away.

I recall hearing Karen Carpenter singing *Rainy Days and Mondays* on the radio one day as we drove back to the facility. The lyrics increased my tears. The song's sense of dull and unspoken powerlessness was a match for my mood.

Even today I can't listen to that song without feeling yet again some of the pain and sadness. And I find it very hard to say good-bye to anyone I love—the residue of my days as an inpatient in that institution. I'm afraid they might not come back to me. When I was little and vulnerable I felt like Karen Carpenter understood what I was facing, although it gave me little comfort.

Arrival with my parents back at the Centre each Sunday evening was ominous. A large dark portrait of a man loomed just inside the Centre's front doors. He may have been the CEO or the founder. For all I know he may have been a kindly man, but to a home-sick young girl who knew she was about to be separated from her family for another five days his portrait was a forbidding presence. The entry hallway to the ward section was dark. It frightened me. When we entered the ward the strong smell of floor cleaner enveloped us. At the nurses' desk a nurse affixed a new hospital bracelet to my wrist and took my temperature.

I then had a few minutes to talk to my parents before they left me there. The hardest thing to endure was kissing them good-bye. As I wrapped my arms in an iron grip around my dad I could smell his Old Spice aftershave lotion. When it was Mom's turn, Chanel #5 perfume enfolded me. No amount of reassurance that they would pick me up again in a few days suppressed my sense that I was being abandoned.

At these times I envied my little brother. He would get to spend the whole week with our mom and dad. I remember thinking: maybe if I could walk they could love me more and maybe they would get me out of there.

I usually cried for the whole ten minutes before a nurse took me away from Mom and Dad, put me in pajamas and then put me into bed. On occasion a nurse took a few minutes to soothe me a little once Mom and Dad had left. Next to the nurses' office there was a fridge with a freezer. The nurse could sometimes find a Popsicle or a freezie in it for me before I was taken to bed. The treat helped cool the tears that poured down my face on these Sunday nights.

During the night in the facility, we were woken at least three times to have our temperatures taken and to be asked to use a bedpan.

At the time I was (like most children) too focused on my own feelings to realize how traumatic my pleadings must have been to my parents. They had been told by the experts of the day that they were doing the right thing for me—but each week on our return to the Centre I was telling them pleadingly that they were doing the wrong thing.

Mom and Dad did what they could to try to lift my spirits. They took me to K-Mart one day when I was six or seven and bought me a doll that looked a little like me. She was beautiful. Brown eyes, long brown hair, a red and white velvet dress, and black shoes. Now I had someone who needed me even when I was in the Crippled Children's Centre.

When I got to the nurses' desk I showed the doll to the nurse in charge. She said, "Let me see her." She lifted up the doll's dress and wrote my first and last name on the doll's back in black permanent marker. She was probably trying to make sure that no one would steal my doll, but I was devastated. My doll was now disabled, just like me. She was now marked as different, at a time when I desperately wanted her—and me—to be like everyone else.

The next weekend my brother and I tried to remove the ink with nail polish remover. It reduced the color on the doll's back but my name was still legible. I threw the doll in the garbage.

The last time I was an inpatient at the Ontario Crippled Children's Centre I was ten years old. I had just had surgery at Sick Kids Hospital to lengthen tendons and muscles in my legs. Medical professionals had convinced my parents that the surgery would straighten my legs and feet, making it easier for me to stand and walk. Post-surgery, I was sent back to the Treatment Centre to endure the lengthy rehabilitation phase. Even though a few years had passed since my last visit, not much had changed except that we could now wear our own clothes.

During that stay the girl in the bed beside me played Edward Bear's tune *Last Song* over and over on the portable record player on her night stand. The song meant much to me. It was about a relationship that had gone bad. Its first verse expressed a boy's hope that his girlfriend would come back.

As I listened repeatedly to the song I closed my eyes and created my own version of it: Mom and Dad, I'm still awake and still my light is on. Please come by and know that I need to come home because I love you, oh yes I do, yes I do…

At ten years old my feeling of isolation while in the Treatment Centre became stronger than it had ever been before. I was acutely aware that I was away from my favorite grade five teacher and all of my school friends. I missed half the school year because of my surgery and rehabilitation, but because I had my school work sent to me and I worked on it whenever I could (even in the middle of the night), I managed to pass Grade 5.

At the age of ten I struggled in other ways too. I was now old enough to realize that I needed to control something in my life—but at first I didn't know how I could do that. Over a few weeks I began to think, "If I stop eating they will have to send me home. I don't like the food here and not eating should be easier to do than most other things I do here." With that thought in mind, I stopped eating. After ten days I overheard the head nurse calling my Mom: "You have to pick her up because she won't eat. All she does is cry. None of that is good for her, so we can't keep her here."

And so I finally went home forever.

I've never spoken in depth to my parents about these periods of institutionalization. Perhaps I felt they needed to be protected from their own painful memories. But I now know they don't need to be protected—they need to be told that their love shone through everything they did for me. I know they made me live in the Treatment Centre for periods of time because they were told that doing so would help me to walk. Like other parents of disabled children, they had to make heart wrenching decisions, imposing pain on their children for the sake of promised long-term gain, decisions that left them questioning everything they thought they knew or understood. I'm sure they felt guilty and trapped at times.

They did everything they could think of to make cherished memories outside of facility walls and to show their love for me. In this they succeeded.

I love them all the more, knowing what they've done for me.

SCHOOL AND THE PRIMACY OF WASHROOMS

School posed a challenge. Conventional wisdom at the time favored segregated schooling for kids with disabilities. Few buildings of any kind were accessible to people with disabilities, and most schools were beyond the reach of a child in a wheelchair.

But my parents' courage, and the stubbornness bred by that courage, convinced them that I would not need to adapt to the reality of inaccessible schools—a school would need to adapt to me.

My father made an agreement with the principal of Springfield School, the local elementary school. He said, "Let her stay here for six months, if she doesn't succeed scholastically, then we will take her out." The principal agreed and I started in kindergarten. My dad told me that I was the first person in Mississauga with a visible disability who was accepted in an elementary school and later in the high school that I attended.

But there were no off-the-shelf wheelchairs to fit someone as small as I was when I started kindergarten. While it may have been possible to have one specially built and designed for me, there weren't a lot of places to get that done and it was likely very costly in 1967 when I was just five years old. So my father, a draftsman who is a whiz at design and innovative construction, built me a wooden chair with four small wheels on it that he found in the basement. He made it small enough for his less than twenty pound daughter. These wheels didn't allow me to move the chair myself, but nevertheless it was a tiny, simple, shiny, brown, wooden mobility device that gave me a way to move around the school, albeit with help from others. I imagine that the school staff didn't think that letting me crawl around the school would be acceptable or safe and they may also have recognized the advantage of having me seated at a height similar to that of my standing class mates.

My chair moved around pretty well on smooth surfaces, but Dad told me not to let people push me around in it quickly. That was fine advice until a classmate in kindergarten started spinning me around in circles one day during recess. I don't think she was being malicious—I think she was just excited to be my chair pusher for that recess. She spun me around too fast and she quickly lost control of the chair. I knew I was about to fall and that I could break bones, and I braced myself. I and the wheelchair survived unscathed, a tribute both to my pliable bones and my dad's construction prowess. The supervising teacher lifted me back into my chair.

By the time I was ready to start grade one, the homemade chair Dad built for his little girl was showing signs of wear and tear, and two of the wheels had started to wobble. Dad disposed of the chair. It was only much later that I came to appreciate the love and skill that he put into its creation.

The chair so lovingly crafted by my dad was replaced by a factory-made wheelchair. It was a very small manual chair called a Tiny Tot. All the metal parts were sparkling chrome, and the seat and backrest were covered in green vinyl. Mom and Dad could easily lift me into it, strap me in with a seatbelt, and place my feet on the footrests. Then I was set to go. The seat was more comfortable then the plain wooden seat in the chair Dad had made for me. I had several other increasingly larger manual wheelchairs as I grew, but in my mind's eye none shone as brightly, greened as greenly or moved as smoothly as my first store-bought chair.

Like most manual wheelchairs, then and now, my chair folded to fit in a car trunk and had a lightly padded foldable fabric seat. Like most manual wheelchairs, mine had push rims attached to the two large rear wheels. It is these push rims, not the tires that the wheelchair driver uses to move the chair. To go forward you need to reach back and grip the push rims as far back as you can. You push the wheels forward by holding the rims and moving them forward. To go backward you reach forward and grip the push rims, and push them backward. Manual wheelchair users build up muscle strength pushing themselves from here to there, but even with considerable muscle, pushing oneself up a hill or a ramp can be quite a feat. I gave up any dream of climbing physical mountains, preferring to climb metaphorical ones instead.

I had seen others propelling their manual chairs so I knew how to do it, but it took a bit of practice for me to learn to coordinate my arm movements to push me in the direction I wanted to go. After a few days of practice, I felt so happy that I could now move myself: I had my first sense of independence.

I can imagine the fear and anxiety (and perhaps irritation) the school staff felt because they had to move me from place to place in kindergarten before I received my drive-myself shiny green chair. After that, they still had to be sure I got from place to place in the school—a worry for them because the tendency at the time (all too common today as well) would have been to see what a child with a disability couldn't do, rather than what they could do.

There were no accessible washrooms or elevators in Springfield School. When I started kindergarten I wasn't concerned about the lack of these amenities. In terms of getting around the place, the schools I attended weren't all that much different from my home.

The whole idea of learning stuff and spending much of each day with other kids excited me. Many youngsters with disabilities are afraid of being singled out, ridiculed, mocked or marginalized by other kids because of their disabilities—a terrible emotional burden for them to bear and overcome when they start school. But the ease with which my family, the neighbors and children in the neighborhood had accepted me "as is" when I was a preschooler (before some of that acceptance was dampened by the culture of the Treatment Centre) made it much easier for me to see school as new opportunities rather than as threats to my self-image.

I actually became a bit of a celebrity in school, because my classmates were keen to take turns pushing me around. At recess I had to stay on the pavement section of the playground because school staff were concerned about getting me onto and off the soft and bumpy field area—so I became the school's specialist in holding and turning skipping ropes for other kids.

Despite my eagerness to embrace the experiences that school offered, I knew I would face practical problems. But even as a crawling toddler I had figured out how to be a problem solver—someone who was innovative, resilient, and very patient. I had built it into my very being (putting a lie to the stereotype of the helpless gimp that many people with mobility disabilities have to deal with). I became a pessimistic optimist—someone who prepares for the worst and hopes for the best.

When was I a pessimistic optimist in elementary school? Every time I had to go to the washroom! Since there were no accessible facilities in the school I had to prepare for my day by making sure that I wouldn't need to go to the washroom until Mom came to the school at 11:45 to take me home for lunch (most students went home for lunch). That meant drinking nothing until lunch time and hoping I wouldn't have an accident on school property. Making it home at lunch time and using a familiar bathroom was a great relief (excuse the pun) and freed me to watch *The Flintstones* on TV—a cherished ritual for me.

But some afternoons I was mortified. Despite my planning and my commitment to a lack of drinking, there would sometimes be a puddle under my desk by the time Mom came to pick me up for lunch. She became adept at using paper towels and Mr. Clean when I had these accidents. Neither she nor anyone at the school ever belittled me for these occurrences—but like all kids I was prone to embarrassment and guilt when the unfortunate but inevitable happened.

Despite these complexities I loved being a student: at school I could do as well or better than many other students despite my disability.

But I didn't do well in math. From grades one to twelve the subject was foreign to me. When I brought math homework home, Dad was the assigned tutor, probably because Mom wasn't much better at the subject than I was, or perhaps she asked Dad to help with that subject because she knew she would later be helping with therapy. But despite my dad's own proficiency with numbers, his eyes glazed over after an hour of trying to make me grasp mathematical concepts. I simply stopped trying to come up with answers, knowing that no matter what I thought was right, my answer would be wrong.

I took my last math class in grade 12. By the end of the last term the math teacher gave me fifty-two percent on my final report card. I'm sure she gave me that barely passing mark so that she didn't have to see me anymore. I don't blame her.

The skills and coping strategies that I developed in elementary school became essential in high school. Woodlands Secondary School was much larger than my elementary school, and like my elementary school it had neither accessible washrooms nor elevators. High school from grade seven to grade thirteen was complicated because students rotated from classroom to classroom with a different teacher for each subject. My new school had two floors and a winding staircase with no fewer than sixty stairs. Changing classes often meant moving from one floor to the other. Before I started attending the high school I had to think about how to be innovative, how to adapt to the challenge of the stairs.

As luck would have it, my first morning class in grade seven was science on the second floor. School started at 9:00 a.m. but Mom drove me to school for 8:00 a.m. that morning so we could get me up those stairs. My parents had already bought me an extra manual wheelchair to be positioned on the second floor for me to use every day once I reached the top of the stairs.

At that time I could get up the stairs by walking up with support. My mom would hold my right arm and walk beside me. There were thin vertical posts attaching the handrail to the stairs so I had to grab each one and use my upper arm strength to help pull my feet up each step. I usually did well on the first ten steps but then I had to sit on a step and rest.

It took me close to an hour to get to the top. For the first fifteen minutes of my science class, I was tired and inattentive after my monumental climb. A few days into high school, I recognized that I could achieve this stair climbing effort only once a day at most, so I asked if I could speak to the vice principal. I told him I had seen some very cute and tall older male students around and I asked him if he knew any that could help me get up and down the stairs several times a day. One day, without any advance warning that a hunk was about to help me, I found myself being carried down stairs after my science class by the captain of the football team. Other teammates made themselves available when I needed to go back up and come down. That was one change I was thrilled to adapt too—I admit feeling quite special when the captain of the football team carried me around! Sadly this heart throbbing arrangement lasted only for the remainder of my first year in high school. After that, all of my classes for a given day either took place entirely on the first or second floor of the school. Alas, my football carriers were gone.

Even in high school, my mom had to come back to the school at lunch time so I could use the washroom. She waited outside my last class of the morning until I wheeled out. She then wheeled me into the bathroom, lifted me into the cubicle and waited in the hallway with my wheelchair. Mom remembers smelling the cigarette smoke and the marijuana fumes that flowed out of there on a daily basis—none of which originated from me.

In seventh grade we had tryouts for *Mary Poppins*, that year's school play. While I didn't expect to get an acting role, I still auditioned. I had never seen an actor in a wheelchair before and I thought it was about time to attack the stereotype that people with disabilities can't be actors. I didn't get a part, but the teacher in charge of the play asked me if I'd like to be part of the makeup team. Since two of my girlfriends were also joining the makeup team, I agreed.

The makeup team spent a month learning makeup application practices. Theatre makeup techniques fascinated me, particularly how makeup is used to age people. Because my disability causes fine-motor dexterity issues I was a little slower than others when applying the makeup on my group of actors, but they quickly helped and adapted by putting the foundation base on by themselves before they became face-to-face with me. Due to their efforts I was able to get the rest of the makeup applied quickly enough.

Two weeks before the play's opening night the teacher in charge of the production told me she had learned that wheelchairs could not be located behind a stage because they presented a safety hazard and for that reason I would have to leave the makeup team.

I went home from school in tears. That night I felt a niggling in my mind that wouldn't go away. It seemed cruelly odd to me that I had only just been told about this rule. Why had I been allowed to take part in the makeup application training course if teachers had prior knowledge that I wasn't permitted to be behind the stage? Predisposed to trust my teachers, I tried hard to suppress my fear that I had been lied to, but the fear didn't go away. For four days my mom and dad didn't make me go to school: they knew I felt betrayed by a teacher I had trusted.

When I returned to school I wanted to tell the vice principal how disappointed I was and ask him why I was not told about the wheelchair rule before I got engaged in the makeup team course. I was still so angry at the production teacher that I couldn't bring myself to talk to her. I knocked on the vice principal's door. I explained what had happened, and I saw the expression on his face change during our conversation. At first he appeared annoyed that I was interrupting his work, followed by surprise and disbelief. After I talked with him and cried a bit, he said, "Thank you Lisa. Let me get back to you." Two hours later I was asked to come back to his office. The VP said, "Lisa, I've done some investigating and there is no truth to what you were told. I'm so sorry! The set construction team would be happy to have you on their team if you would like."

I simply shook my head. I was being offered a well-meaning token consolation prize, but I wasn't interested in a token. My joy and excitement at being part of this school-wide event was gone. It took me several weeks to feel happy in school again. The pain that came from being lied to by someone in a position of authority took a long time to fade completely.

Later I learned that the teacher in charge of the makeup team had been suspended for a period of time.

Two silver linings came out of that experience. The first silver lining was my long-term interest in makeup. By asking for information and advice at makeup counters in stores and by watching infomercials on TV, I learned more about makeup application. By the time I got to university I was able to share my learnings with my fellow students.

The second silver lining was my knowledge that my vice principal had stood up for me. Too often, people with disabilities who speak up for their rights, who complain about the service they receive or who merely make genial positive suggestions, are met with explanations provided by people in authority about why things are the way they are, why things can't change, why we should simply be satisfied with the truncated attention society has chosen to give us. Sometimes these defenses of the status quo are delivered to us with a kind of tongue-clucking sympathy: "I really wish we could help, and if it was up to me I would love to help, but I'm afraid we can't."

But one day many years ago, one vice principal took my side, and acted on my behalf. It helped me to believe that people really can act on the basis of justice rather than expedience.

By eighth grade I was able to use the specialized transit services provided by the Region of Peel to get home from school. This gave Mom a much needed break from making a third trip to the school each day. But as I started to use the service, I wondered if I had been an impatient person in a former life. The service operated then (as it does now) using a shared-ride model, so other passengers were often picked up by the bus before it arrived at my school. While school ended at 3:15 p.m. I often had to wait inside the front entrance of the school for an hour or more for my ride home.

The wait was always a crap shoot: on any given afternoon I didn't know if my wait would be ten minutes long, or ten times longer. Weather and traffic problems also led to pick up delays. By 4:30 or 5:00 p.m., if I was still waiting for my transportation I often yearned for the washroom—but I couldn't abandon my waiting spot in case the bus arrived while I was in the washroom and left without me.

When people ask me what have been the biggest barriers I've faced because of my disability, I say access to accessible washrooms and reliable, timely transportation.

I promise to abandon the topic of washrooms after this section, but given that they are essential for all people and such a massive barrier for people who use wheelchairs, please indulge me in my rant.

It never automatically occurs to me to drink anything even though, all my life, I have been advised by medical professionals and other people to drink more water. I consciously limit my fluid intake every time I go anywhere because of my anxiety about getting into a washroom, be it accessible or not. This means that visits to locations like new restaurants, movie theatres or offices can be stressful.

In the eighties, regulators decided that raised toilet seats should be put into most accessible washrooms along with (in some situations) grab bars on the wall that angle downwards. I was told that the raised toilet seats were installed to assist people who might be helping someone onto and off of the toilet. The helpers would not have to bend down so low when helping someone. O. K., sounded good! It had also been determined that wheelchair users need more space in washrooms to maneuver their chairs. With more space I could at least bring myself and my chair into washrooms. However, trying to use them without falling proved to be a monumental task. Angled-down grab bars probably help people with some capacity to stand independently. I try to grip them near the top to ensure that I remain standing as I transfer myself from my chair to the toilet, but inevitably my hand slides down and I struggle to ensure that I don't end up sitting half undressed on the bathroom floor.

Then I need to ensure I can get onto the toilet. As a five foot woman I have a limited capacity to land safely on a toilet seat that is at least five inches higher than a standard low toilet. When I successfully make the transfer I am often still anxious because my feet don't touch the floor and the possibility of falling is real. So a policy meant to make it easier for some people to use toilets, and easier for their helpers to lift them, proves a disadvantage to other people with disabilities.

I wonder if anyone calculated the average height of wheelchair users before mandating raised toilet seats.

Washrooms often make it difficult or impossible for me to close the cubicle door once I'm inside the cubicle. That's because most often the door opens outward and doesn't close automatically. This means I would have to back into the washroom so I can close the door, or turn my wheelchair around 180 degrees inside the cubicle to close the door, or (implausibly enough) reach over my shoulder to close the door. When I get close enough to the grab bar, I am too far away from the door to reach it, close it and lock it. As a consequence there are times when I have to use public washrooms with the door left open. The need to use the facilities sometimes outweighs the need or opportunity for privacy.

Sometimes in smaller washrooms the door swings inward into the cubicle, presumably so it will not bash an unsuspecting fellow washroom user when it is opened. However the inward-swinging door cuts down on available space in the cubicle, making it hard or impossible to maneuver a wheelchair into the right position for the user to reach the grab bar.

I have many good friends who routinely help me with this stuff as a matter of course. They all exude kindness and respect toward me as they help. The man to whom I am connected is very much like that. He will stand outside a ladies' washroom and if he senses that I am taking too long or am perhaps struggling, he will enter the washroom and say something like: "Excuse me ladies, I need to get in there to help my partner. When you can, would you please vacate for a few minutes?"

For me and for many other people with disabilities, the fear of falling in a strange washroom has at least three dimensions. One is the possibility of injury, since washrooms aren't noted for soft floors and cushioned walls. Another is the embarrassment of sprawling on the floor in the nearby presence of other people. Yet a third is anxiety about whether strangers will be nearby to help and whether they will be willing and able to help. Some wonderful women have helped me in those situations—but some have scurried way, mumbling a parting apology, rather than helping. Some (very few I'm glad to say), neither helping nor leaving, have merely gawked at a curious fallen fellow human.

In the early 90s I was keynote speaker at a conference for women with disabilities who were considering becoming parents. I noticed a young woman in the audience who had a slogan-button on her wheelchair that said, "Everyone deserves the right to pee."

I and other people with disabilities understand the message.

Lest I seem like a mere complainer, someday I, the cautious optimist, will find the perfect public washroom. This is what it will look like:

- The door to the washroom itself has a button-activated automatic opener.
- There are at least two accessible cubicles. One has a higher toilet seat, one has a lower seat. The kind of seat is marked on each cubicle's door.
- The cubicle door swings outward. When it is in the open position, it gently swings into the closed position thirty seconds after it was opened.
- There is plenty of room in the cubicle to maneuver a wheelchair.

- There is a properly sized grab bar that has a sloping arm, a vertical arm and a horizontal arm to it, to accommodate a variety of users.
- The floor is not wet or littered with paper that can precipitate a slip or fall.
- The area immediately around the toilet is textured with a non-slip surface.
- Each sink is high enough for a user to get a wheelchair close to it, and the counter shallow enough that wheelchair users don't need to reach too far to operate the accessible faucet handles.
- The cubicle contains an ATM machine that dispenses unlimited free cash to people in wheelchairs (I'm kidding about this one).

One piece of advice to my walking readers: since you can walk, please don't use the wheelchair accessible washroom cubicle. If there is a long line in the washroom, you are desperate and the cubicle is empty by all means go ahead and use it. Just be quick. Those of us who use mobility aids have no other option apart from the accessible cubicle, but you do have other facilities you can use.

I REFUSE. I BECOME.

In 1975 I turned thirteen and I made a life-changing decision. I decided that I was going to stop trying to learn to walk. I knew that even if I could eventually walk I would never be able to do it with the stamina, grace, and ease that becomes second nature to kids who learn to walk in the first eighteen months of their lives.

I made that choice at a time when I had grown tired of a life that consisted primarily of going to school, coming home to do homework, and taking part in a repetitive daily ritual of physiotherapy sessions that seemed to last forever. This therapeutic "make-me-better" process had become all-encompassing, degrading, and humiliating without producing immediate visible benefits.

Because adults presented walking as an essential life-altering skill that would transform me into a complete human being, I never felt that I was given the option to focus on much else. I became desperate to share experiences with others who, like me, were young and grappling with the challenges of determining who we were as young people and who we hoped to become as we matured.

I also knew I was falling behind others of my own age in acquiring normal teenage street knowledge and developing the confidence and skills that help kids to become self-assured adults.

So I decided not to walk, not to waste hours learning to stagger from one support to another simply to achieve a semblance of what everyone else did with ease. And this decision rammed me head on into society's assumption that cripples like me would want to sacrifice just about anything for the sake of learning to walk.

This choice didn't suddenly pop into my head. It was a long-drawn out decision. As a very young girl, I aimed to please my parents. I never wanted to disappoint them. My desire to please became even stronger when I went to school—an environment I embraced, but where I nevertheless faced daily reminders that I was not the same as other kids. So I kept trying to learn to walk. I didn't want to be different. As if it was a mathematical axiom, I accepted the message that I had been told repeatedly by so many people. If I learned to walk, I could be just like other kids. Lisa, plus walking, equals normal. And I wanted to make my mom and my dad proud of me. I wanted to be their normal daughter.

But an intense discontent began to grow within me. Eventually it surfaced, seeping into every part of my thoughts and feelings. I began to understand that for the first twelve years of my life I had observed the world from within the confines of a highly structured daily routine over which I had no say. Too often my life focused on therapy rather than on living. I watched how life was changing and influencing other kids. I needed to be part of the process of growing up and asserting my independence.

Once I decided that I would have a full life whether I walked or not, I stopped talking to my mom during the therapy sessions. Then over time, I gradually shut down even more and I stopped being the readily compliant child. I eventually refused to do the exercises. I finally told my mom why I resisted the therapy. We argued heatedly with each other about my decision.

I never talked to my dad about this because he was not the parent who initiated or acted as the overseer and participant in the forever therapy sessions. He was a 60s and 70s father, braver than most in defending me for sure, but he nevertheless focused on being an excellent provider for his family, leaving therapy up to my mom. I can recall Dad attending some assessment meetings mandated by professionals to discuss me and my progress or lack of it. I suspect that he went to help support Mom: she often emerged from those sessions in tears, feeling she had failed as a parental therapist or even as a parent. I can only imagine the pain she felt when supposed experts told her I probably wouldn't amount to much.

I'm sure my mother was perplexed and frightened by my new-found stubbornness. For years, professionals told her that walking was the only way I would be equal to others and accepted in the world. But when she could no longer get me to work towards that goal, she eventually stopped demanding that I "just do it". I don't know if Mom finally called Ontario Crippled Children's Centre and said, "I just can't bring this kid back to you." She did something at some point, because all therapy eventually stopped. When that happened, she gradually relaxed a little. She was no longer regularly subjected to hearing from professionals the insidious under-message that she was being a less than perfect mom.

One day, when our fights and disagreements about mandatory therapy had abated, I simply said: "OK Mom, I love you, and now that I'm done with therapy, I gotta start having a teenage life." She looked frightened when I said this but she accepted my decision and she gradually supported me in a thousand ways as I followed my path to greater independence. I'm proud to say she finally embraced more than my decision—she embraced the reality that I, like all other teenagers, would have to climb over the wreckage of my own mistakes rather than being sheltered from them.

I didn't know how important my decision to be a wheelie rather than a walkie would be, but within days of making it I began experiencing both the subtle and the more obvious impacts of this decision. I began to develop deeper insights into how the world perceives people with disabilities.

The Me People See

I had already learned that if you sit in a wheelchair, people will judge you in ways that people who walk are never judged.

Some people will stare—not the wide-eyed innocent stare of a child (a stare that I welcome because the child may be learning for the first time that people in wheelchairs exist) —but a stare verging on resentment that I've made myself visible in their world.

Some people will assume that I suffer from an incurable disease, on an express train (or an express wheelchair) toward early death. They're already fitting me for a coffin and a halo. If they admit to this assumption, it gives me great pleasure to let them know that cerebral palsy is a condition, not a terminal illness, and that I will be around for quite some time.

Some believe I have an infectious disease. A few times mothers with children have crossed to the other side of the street rather than pass by me on the sidewalk, presumably so I won't infect their kids. After I graduated from university I vacationed with some friends in Jamaica. We attended a church service on Easter Sunday while we were there. After the service, the minister told me that I could hang one hundred dollars bills off myself and no one there would touch them. When I asked why, he said, "Because people here will be afraid of catching what you have." This fear is by no means limited to Jamaica. But at least in Jamaica someone had the guts to admit it.

Some will say unkind things, dismissive things, ignorant things. Some will assume or suggest that you can't do something. If your chair is a power chair rather than a manual one, you will likely be considered even less able, despite the skills you exhibit as you navigate this heavy hunk of technology through a hazard-strewn world. And the ambulatory world most often views a wheelchair as something that those of us with mobility disabilities are "confined to", "bound to" or "tied to". These phrases are part of what columnist Michael Gerson calls "the soft bigotry of low expectations"—a form of bigotry that lacks the barbed malice of more aggressive forms, but that can still imprison people living with disabilities.

My reality has been that my chairs have all allowed me to achieve and savor independence. A wheelchair does not bind you. Instead, these wheels help users to participate in life. They provide us with skills and strategies—just as valuable as the skills and strategies involved in walking—that carry us through our lives.

I learned early that I would be subjected to comments about aspects of my life that appear on the surface to be compliments, but that are in fact rooted in an underestimation of the lives of people with disabilities. Even forty-one years after my life-changing decision was made, these "complimentary insults" leave me scratching my head:

> "You're really cute/smart/pretty/sexy—for someone in a wheelchair."

> "You are so inspiring!"

> "I could never be as brave as you are."

> "Seeing a lovely girl like you in a wheelchair just makes me want to cry."

> "What a tragedy! Can't they cure you?"

People have said these things to me. And people with disabilities are also aware of the unsaid things. They know there is still a too common misconception that people in wheelchairs are unattractive, dirty, sloppy, and stupid. Even a supposed complement that implies I am not as deficient as other gimps is a backhanded compliment, something that would be an insult were it not rooted in stereotypes.

Many of the people I know in chairs are very attractive and intelligent, but that's not the relevant issue. If you are going to compliment someone, that's great! Just leave the chair out of it.

After years of being in a chair, I don't want to be called inspiring for choosing to live my life. I am not remarkable just because I have developed ways to accomplish the day to day tasks that others also do. I suspect that some people call me inspiring after noticing my mobility limitations and seeing how the environment that we all live in doesn't do enough to make my challenges easier. They may also think to themselves, "If I were in your situation, I couldn't possibly do what you are doing."

I believe that almost any life challenge, disability-related or otherwise, provides the challenged person with the capacity to become a creative problem solver. If we all want to get a rich array of experiences from our lives, we each need to figure out how to make them happen despite our limitations. It is a great life lesson to realize that you need to enjoy the things in life that are possible and recognize that none of us will be as independent in our old age as we were when we were younger.

Everyone will need help at some point. Some people, who have not yet had this insight take their capacity for granted and believe that the abilities they have now will continue forever. Based on that belief, it is understandable that these folks have not yet had to develop or draw on their innate capacity to find solutions to challenges. Creative problem solving becomes second nature to long-term wheelchair users as we regularly cope with personal and environmental change—but this is not a characteristic specific to people with disabilities. It is specific to anyone facing a challenge, and that means just about everybody.

"Poor brave dear, you must suffer terribly."

This stereotype assumes that my life comprises misery because I can't walk. Its tongue-clucking sympathy denies me, in the eyes of the beholder, the possibility of joy, of triumph, or of even a commonplace boring day. At its most insidious it implies that my supposed suffering ennobles and empowers me and makes me a "magical cripple"—a term I adapt from the phrase "magical Negro" popularized by film director Spike Lee. In literary criticism, the magical Negro is a character who, by use of special insight or powers, helps a more prominent white character to get out of trouble, but who generally has few meaningful characteristics of their own.

I am not a magical cripple. I am simply me.

In addition to stereotypes masking as compliments, there are stereotypes that assume I can be made more normal if only I behaved differently. For example:

"With enough prayer and effort you will be able to walk."

This message assumes that walking is an essential human capacity and that without the ability to walk a person isn't whole or complete.

Walking ability is rarely acquired solely through prayer and effort. At least in my situation, it just didn't work that way. A microwave oven that has not been programmed or has not been plugged-in or has been damaged will not function no matter how much effort a person puts in to making it work. Far better to find a workable alternative to the microwave, as I did in my life.

Intense sustained effort on my part did not make me walk! And if I were to ask of anything from God as a kind of cosmic Christmas present, I wouldn't ask for a new neurological system. I might, however, ask for a wheelchair with helicopter blades.

Another set of stereotypes equates the disability, or the ability aid, with the person—in effect, burying the person beneath one visible manifestation of their life. An example:

"We need a table for five people and a wheelchair."

Early in my professional working life our executive director wanted to acknowledge our efforts after a particularly challenging team project and we all wanted to relax and enjoy lunch at a local restaurant. The greeter at the door of our chosen restaurant signaled our arrival by shouting to our server-to-be, "We need a table for five people and a wheelchair."

On that day the very device that facilitated my freedom and independence was personified. I didn't exist as a person. I was the wheelchair.

I am not, and never have been, my wheelchair. It is simply the device that I use to facilitate my mobility.

The offensive comment so disturbed one of my colleagues that she berated the offending greeter. As for me, I was still struggling to be accepted as a fully capable and resourceful employee, unwilling to draw unnecessary attention to myself, so I ignored what the greeter had said. But to this day I remain grateful for my co-worker's response, and herein lies another lesson. People with disabilities do not always need the help of others. But when I need help (as everyone needs help from time to time), and that help is offered, I should accept it with grace and thanks.

I'm also gratified when a walkie expresses matter-of-fact insight into the nature of disability. All the better if that individual is someone famous enough to influence many others—a person like Fred Rogers, who pointed out that part of the problem with the word "disabilities" is that it immediately suggests an inability to see or hear or walk or do other things that many of us take for granted. But what of people who can't feel? Or talk about their feelings? Or manage their feelings in constructive ways? What of people who aren't able to form close and strong relationships? And people who cannot find fulfillment in their lives or those who have lost hope, who live in disappointment and bitterness, and find in life no joy, no love? These, it seemed to Fred Rogers, are the real disabilities.

It has been important to me throughout my life to avoid developing my own stereotypes. I constantly struggle to remember, for example, that people who hold preconceived notions about people with disabilities are not implacably hostile, and that their views can be changed. And on days when I feel—as we all do from time to time—that fate is treating me unfairly, I struggle to remember the words of the nineteenth century theologian Theodore Parker:

> "Look at the facts of the world. You see a continual and progressive triumph of the right. I do not pretend to understand the moral universe, the arc is a long one, and my eye reaches but little ways. I cannot calculate the curve and complete the figure by the experience of sight;

I can divine it by conscience. But from what I see I am sure it bends towards justice."

I'm not a missionary whose every word preaches inclusion, nor am I a magical cripple destined to teach others. I am merely Lisa Jones, trying to get through the day with a little joy, hope, kindness, and humor. Just like everybody else.

REVERSAL

I'm glad you're still reading this book. But lest your weary eyelids begin to close as a result of my sermonizing in the previous chapter, let me change the pace by sharing with you a short story I wrote and entered into a writing competition recently.

I didn't win, but that doesn't matter. The act of writing it allowed me to indulge to a bit of science fiction—a genre well suited to hide within it our universal human need to create parables. It also highlights fears that I myself would feel if I could suddenly walk now, even for a short time.

Here goes…..

"Gentlemen, we can rebuild him. We have the technology. We have the capability to build the world's first bionic man. Steve Austin will be that man. Better than he was before. Better, stronger, faster."

Better, stronger, faster, the new improved human crafted by the TV show *The Six Million Dollar Man* in 1974, still replayed himself in Faith's head. There was only a small variation to the narration. "We can re-build her. We have the technology."

She wanted a child. To make motherhood and child care easier she was considering undergoing selective dorsal rhizotomy surgery. This procedure involves cutting sensory nerve fibers that run from muscles to the spinal cord. Cutting the right nerves would reduce the number of messages sent from muscles to the brain, reducing spasticity and allowing this woman with cerebral palsy to walk if it worked. It was experimental and a big "If". But, she reasoned, it could make it so much easier to care for my child, and I can finally dump the damned wheelchair.

Steve Austin entered her mind again as she lay on the operating table counting backwards from ten. She could see him becoming bigger, stronger, faster, just as the show had promised. A smile etched her face as her eyes closed. A few hours later there was only pain, so her eyes closed again. Over the next two weeks the pain subsided, getting on and off the bed gradually got easier and standing up supported by a walker became possible. In the regulated little world of the hospital, everything seemed to progress nicely. And Faith was not the kind of person who would play "what if?" with herself. So when her husband Paul came to pick her up, a nurse helped her into her own wheelchair and wheeled her out of the main door. "Faith, you were a model patient. Don't forget to rely on your walker for support. Good luck!"

As their car approached the driveway, Faith saw her first mountain—the three steps leading up to the front door of her house. For a moment she considered getting back into her wheelchair and getting inside the house by going up the ramp that was set up along the side of the house. But almost immediately, she heard the recurring and insistent babble of voices in her head that took delight in highlighting the many reasons why she would experience disappointment and failure. To suppress this, her own tentative voice spoke.

"Paul, please just put the chair and the walker in the garage. I'll use the steps."

Tentatively and hoping to display more confidence then she actually felt, she grasped the stair railing bolted to the wall of the house. She was surprised to discover that it wobbled. Pulling hard on it, she leaned forward and willed her right foot to make it up the first step but nothing happened. After several tries she remembered what her therapist had said at the hospital: "Keep your body upright, don't lean forward, press the stair away with your stronger foot, and move the other leg to the next step." Fear, sweat, and anxiety about which foot was stronger preceded that effort, but after twenty minutes she was in her house. Breathing heavily, she sat down on a kitchen chair for a few minutes while Paul put the coffee on. She wished that her walker was inside, but to ask Paul to bring it to her would admit to failure. She knew that confident walking would take time. The limitations imposed by the walker re-surfaced. Learning to use the walker had resulted in severe pressure through her arms and into her hands. Red and inflamed indentations had left patterns on her hands that still remained.

Using the walker also meant that her arms and hands were otherwise occupied, so any other necessary activity would be out of the question. Faith did not have any idea how she could ever move herself and her baby around independently and safely using this device.

She stood up and walked slowly down the hall to the kitchen. By pressing each of her elbows against both sides of the wall as she walked she was able to maintain her balance. Paul had picked up groceries while she was in hospital and had put some of them on shelves she had not previously been able to reach. Faith took some of them out of the fridge and some from the now-reachable shelves and began making dinner. From her ambulatory position she could see that the top of the fridge needed a good cleaning. "If I was eight feet tall," she mused, "lord knows how many dusty places I could see in this house."

Sitting down on a chair at the kitchen table she chopped up the salad ingredients and assembled the chicken and rice casserole. Paul helped her put the fixings in the oven: with her poor balance, bending to open the oven door and lifting a heavy baking dish inside would guarantee a fall.

Having had to stand, walk, and sit many times just to prepare the dinner, her lower back and legs (from hips to toes), unaccustomed to repeated alien movements, screamed in pain. She realized she had been able to do these tasks more easily while she was safely seated in her wheelchair. She was exhausted and aching, and unexpectedly flooded with tears. It wasn't supposed to be this hard, she thought—Steve Austin wouldn't have found it this hard. Steve Austin wouldn't cry.

After a few minutes she also began to think about the impact that her "improved mobility" might have on her relationship with Paul. He had always easily accepted her disability and was always willing and able to get them both comfortable and functional in bed. She wondered how his expectations would change now that she was supposed to have the capacity and stamina to do more. That night, in bed, she fell asleep in Paul's arms. She hadn't been able to tell him why she had cried, why standing and walking seemed to lead her to a world of new hurdles. Paul did not press her. He knew she was in a new found world and hadn't yet found the words to talk about it.

As the weeks passed, Faith walked short, careful distances unaided. She looked up videos of people walking to try to get some idea of how the natural process felt. She still couldn't figure out what to do with her arms and tended to leave them stiff, like a toy soldier's arms, at her sides, or splayed outward like pathetic thin wings to stabilize her. She still felt like she was practicing a dance that much of the world knew but she did not. For years she and Paul had shared a joke: they were a mixed marriage, one walkie and one wheelie. Now they were both walkies. But one of them would always be better at it than the other.

Every daily task still required time and monumental energy, even after she had figured out how best to accomplish it from a non-sitting position. Her shoulders also still provided daily aching and ongoing reminders that she had pushed herself in a manual wheelchair for too many years and used her arms as both her arms and legs for a long time. Some of the changes that had been made in her house to accommodate her wheelchair were too low now to give her much help.

Being able to stand made it easier to do things like clean windows and open and close curtains. She no longer had to accept wet wheelchair tire marks as a standard component of the freshly mopped kitchen floor.

In the early part of the winter Faith and Paul went to their favorite restaurant to celebrate their anniversary. When Faith asked their waiter for wine, he said, "Are you sure you should have more? Your walking was unsteady when you guys came in."

She thought of letting the waiter know she was a newly minted walker. "But no," she decided, "I'm tired of explaining myself."

The drive back home took a while: it had started to snow and the unsalted roads were slippery. On the driveway, Paul said: "O.K. sweetheart, let me take in the groceries, and I'll come back and help you into the house." Faith waited for a couple of minutes, but as she was getting cold, she decided to step out of the car. She felt her leg slide under her body.

When she opened her eyes she heard the ER doctor speaking to Paul: "I don't think she will be able to walk again. All of the muscles and ligaments are torn and the leg is broken. I'm sorry, but you'll need to bring her wheelchair here when she's able to go home."

Faith smiled as her eyes closed again.

UNIVERSITY EXPERIENCES

Despite my uncomfortable memories of my time as an inpatient in the Ontario Crippled Children's Centre when I was a young girl, I decided in 1980, at the age of eighteen, to go back there once a week for two months to learn to drive. The Centre had acquired cars that operated with hand controls so people with disabilities could learn to drive. I took the in-class part of the course and passed it easily.

After a few weeks we were ready to begin learning the actual task of driving. When my mother delivered me for the first lesson, one of the classroom assistants (a physiotherapist), said to her, "Um, just so you know, our experience with people with cerebral palsy shows us that they can't really drive well. They don't control their spasms and they often don't have enough dexterity to drive safely."

I could feel my heart and my hope for greater mobility sinking. But at that time, in good dry weather I could get myself into a car fairly easily, so I decided to continue with the lessons. Each student received a half hour one-on-one session with a driving instructor once a week for eight weeks. Like the rest of my classmates with disabilities I was pretty nervous the first time I tried to drive so I didn't do a great job. I went back for another driving class but I sensed that the instructors were just putting up with me as well as with some of the other students. It seemed they had already decided that some of us simply could not get licensed.

When winter arrived I found out that I couldn't safely transfer from my wheelchair to the driver's seat in snowy weather, so I looked into the possibility of buying a wheelchair accessible van in which controls such as the brakes and accelerator were operated by hand rather than by foot. But because not a lot of vehicle modifications had been done up to then, it would have cost me at least $14,000 to customize a van to meet my needs, in addition to the cost of the vehicle.

I had worked as a playground supervisor in Mississauga during the summers when I was 16 and 17 and I had saved most of my earnings to help pay my university tuition. So I had a choice—buy a van and customize it, or pay to go to university.

I chose university, a choice made easier by my parents' kindness in agreeing to help pay for it.

In 1981 Carleton University in Ottawa accepted me as a student. It was one of the most accessible universities in eastern Canada, its location in a bilingual city would give me the opportunity to improve my French, and I would be able to make frequent visits to my mom's family in Ottawa. I intended to learn to be a journalist. As a young girl I loved reading and writing. I thought that if I became a journalist I could document events in my own creative way. I quickly found out that journalism's rules were quite strict and not very flexible.

For my first year I lived in residence with two graduate students. I was allowed to bunk with them because they lived in a suite and their rooms were bigger than the undergraduate ones, providing sufficient room for my wheelchairs and me. I used a power wheelchair during classes because the university connected its course locations via underground tunnels and the power chair made it possible to get through tunnels to my classes on time. In our suite I used my manual wheelchair.

My first roommates and I connected very quickly. To this day none of the three of us can explain how we all became so easily and totally connected within two weeks. One of my roommates was from Hong Kong. She was working on a Master's in social work. The other roommate, from Winnipeg, was working on a Master's in journalism. Years later this woman told me that she had been very anxious when she first encountered me: I was the first person she had ever met who used a wheelchair. Her anxiety was heightened by my mom, who herself was anxious about leaving me at Carleton. Shortly after I checked in to our suite my mom approached her and said, "Would you be able to help my daughter if she needs help in the washroom?" That was an unexpected and scary question posed to someone who had never known someone who used a wheelchair but my mother, my beloved protector, had learned throughout my life to be blunt and forward when I needed help.

Despite their initial fears and concerns about how best to lend me a hand, both my roommates soon started to help me out when I needed it. Neither of these lovely women ever showed the slightest sign that they saw me an imposition. The three of us became life-long friends despite that unnerving introduction.

The residence also provided me with the help of a personal care attendant who came to my room for about an hour and a half every morning so I could shower and dress fairly quickly.

At first I found it hard to accept this help. I hadn't yet learned to accept help as gracefully as I do now. When I lived at home I carried out as much personal care as possible on my own, although it took up a lot of my morning time. My mom helped when I couldn't do something by myself. Now that I was in university I couldn't spare the time to get ready for the day without help.

But now, rather than getting help from a family member, I would need to rely on a paid stranger. I felt I was relinquishing my personal independence and privacy. But the attendants who helped me were not strangers for very long, and their help allowed me to retain the energy I needed to experience a full academic and social life on campus.

I also relied on the patience of my roommates, since there were now four women who needed to use the bathroom each morning, and I and my attendant were the gluttonous duo who used it the longest. My roommates showed a lot of forbearance each morning. We more than muddled through.

I was always academically driven, but I had my share of fun as well. When my roommates and I took a break from academic work, we most often found something to do together. Sometimes our relaxation involved simply sitting on the couch in our suite, alone or with others from our floor, talking, and sharing wine. Other times we went together to concerts, movies, or comedy shows in the pubs on campus. The fact that all three of us came from places far away from the university meant that we couldn't go home on the weekends. This helped to knit us together.

One weekend my roommate said she wanted to make homemade Chinese food for the three of us. We were excited about that because we wanted to try Chinese food that didn't come from a Chinese restaurant, and we needed a break from the repetitive food in our cafeteria. She had gone to a nearby Asian grocery store earlier in the week and bought the fixings for our private feast. She left them in a student refrigerator located on our floor. Late on Saturday afternoon she plugged in her rice cooker and an electric frying pan and left them on the coffee table in our suite. We went to the small student kitchen. After a minute I heard her say, "Oh no!" She took something wrapped in plastic out of the fridge and showed it to us. Someone had eaten most of the raw pork sausage she had bought. Our homemade dinner was cancelled because we'd been robbed of its key ingredient and we were left wondering how sick the person who ate the raw sausage had become. We never did find out. We were content with a pizza that night.

Since then I've had opportunities to enjoy Chinese food cooked by this good friend. When I used to eat meat, her soya sauce chicken was one of my absolute favorites! Even today I think of her cooking as my gold standard for Chinese food. No restaurant has ever met that standard.

The three of us were like sisters living together. We helped each other with our school work and we supported each other through experiences that were good, bad or ugly. The immediate respect, love, and support that all three of us fostered in my first year at Carleton enriched my life and remains vivid in my memory.

By my second year at Carleton, my wonderful first year roommates had finished their Masters programs and had left Carleton. I missed them terribly. Even today, although we live too far apart to see each other regularly, we reconnect from time to time. Each time we find ourselves effortlessly transported back to our university days or into the interesting details of the lives we lead now.

I was moved to a different suite with two new roommates. None of us had roomed together before. Our relationship developed in a positive but more typical roommate way: while we got along well and respected each other, we didn't develop strong or lasting connections.

For my third year at Carleton I lived off campus with two friends in an apartment. It was close to the university and it was relatively easy to wheel back and forth. I had decided to leave residence after my second year because I was about to tackle the most demanding school year and I wanted to leave the noisy campus world. All three of us living together used wheelchairs and my male and female housemates after a short time married each other.

On one occasion, having fun turned out to be a wonderful exercise in creativity on the part of people around me. A classmate who lived with her parents near the university asked me if I wanted to go skating on the Rideau Canal near the Carleton campus. People could skate for miles on the canal. I pointed out to her that I couldn't skate. "Yes you can," she said. "Just wait and see."

With the help of canal supervisory staff I was put into my manual wheelchair and lowered onto the canal's ice surface. I was tilted back in my chair while long metal runners that looked like skis were placed under my wheelchair wheels from front to back on both sides. My wheels were tied securely to the metal pieces so they couldn't move. When the runners were attached my friend put on her skates and pushed me all over the canal, while a canal supervisor stayed nearby. Many other skaters took a few curious peeks at us, as we worked together to figure out how to make this new form of locomotion work. It's fair to say that the event damaged my friends' skates a bit. Even so, it was an hour of great fun—until she got tired and I got cold.

It didn't lead to a career for me as a professional skater.

On some weekends when I didn't have a ton of homework, I went to my aunt's home to visit her and my two cousins, a boy five years younger than me and a girl ten years younger than me. The visits gave us all an opportunity to chat and a chance for me to break away from my typewriter for a few hours and to enjoy a homemade meal. Those visits also cemented a lasting bond between me, my aunt and my cousins.

University was a liberal and accepting environment for me. While there still weren't tons of people with disabilities there, at least some of us had made it to the university and there was a general acceptance of people from many backgrounds and cultures. Not all students or professors shared that mindset, but I sensed that the university culture fostered tolerance and interest in people. The university's academic environment also led me to realize that everything we thought we knew should be open to question, analysis, and debate.

In my third year at Carleton I was allowed to take a fourth year French course because I had taken French, English, German, and Spanish in high school and done well in these courses. My university French professor was a warm and inviting woman, proud of the efforts students made to speak and write French well. By her example she taught me an important lesson about teaching: it is more important to take pride in the accomplishments of one's students than to take pride in your own efforts to teach.

In addition to (and sometimes instead of) scholastics, partying, drinking, and sex were top priorities for many students. While I was there to do some serious studying, I too took part in those activities. There was an unspoken understanding that many students didn't want to end their undergraduate years as virgins, so connecting simply for sexual experiences was accepted. The student infirmary recognized this: they handed out birth control pills and condoms like candy. My connections with three young men were short-term and without much emotional meaning. While I liked all three and they were sweet and kind to me, there was no love involved and I always drank enough alcohol to ensure that I didn't wake up knowing much about the experiences we had been through. Like many other students I just wanted to check that experience off my list. I realized after the encounters that I hadn't learned anything significant about human closeness and love. I had not gleaned any real knowledge about how to please a man or be pleased in return, and I had no sense of whether I was actually loved or hated based on my disability. That said, I did what there was to do.

The scholastic component of my university life was heavy and time consuming. I often spent two or three days in the same clothes because the demands of my courses and timelines didn't allow for much sleep.

After the first semester of year one, I dropped out of the journalism program because I couldn't tolerate writing everything in a specific style. For me at least, this disciplined form of writing stifled creativity. I then took an extra night class during the rest of my first school year as I was late leaving journalism and signing up for my undergrad degree in English and psychology instead of journalism.

I thought that if journalism wasn't for me, perhaps I could become a great teacher. I was attracted to the art of helping insights to bloom in the minds of young people. I believed I had the patience, the observational skills and the internal discipline necessary to teach. I picked up an undergrad degree with two majors, one in English and psychology, in hope of becoming a teacher.

After I made this decision I learned about a unique opportunity offered as part of my psychology degree. If students worked hard and completed all their academic courses early, they could be selected to participate in a psychology practicum placement that would use up more than fifty percent of the total time usually necessary just to obtain the psychology degree. I decided to take summer school courses every year while I was at Carleton in the hope that I would be chosen for one of the practicum placements. By taking summer courses I achieved a higher than expected grade point average and I also reduced my academic workload for the following year.

I completed all of my academic psychology requirements in less than three years' time, and I was chosen for the practicum placement. My psychology professor recommended me to an elementary school in Ottawa that was seeking extra help in a specific classroom. Along with eleven of my other classmates I became a volunteer teacher's assistant in a school. Each of us was assigned to a different school. I worked directly with two students from January to June of 1983. One was a little boy who was labelled as intellectually disabled and the second was a little girl who was labelled as gifted. Both children were six years old and both were in grade one.

My role was to research the psychological impacts that students with these labels would face, understand the impacts of their behavior on the other students and find ways to integrate them into normal classrooms. It was fairly easy to do these things for the gifted girl. I created reading and math learning tasks for her that were at the grade four level. She quickly acquired skills at that level but when she was asked to read or do math in front of other students she pretended that she could only do it at their level or that she didn't know what to do at all. She knew that most children couldn't do what she could at her age, and she was afraid they would see her as a show-off. This lovely little girl reminded me yet again how eager I had been—how eager we all are—to be like others, even if it means hiding important and unique parts of ourselves.

For the little boy, my job was to help him to sit with other students during story time for at least ten minutes, help him to try something academic in school every day and prevent him from lashing out at other students. The teacher told me that other students had become afraid of him.

I asked his mom what his favorite treats were. On the first day that I was with him, I arrived with a sack full of these treats—gummy bears and colored pencils. Initially I said to the teacher that I would give him one gummy for every two minutes that he sat listening during story time, provided that he also managed to avoid touching any other student who was listening. I showed the little guy how to look at the minute hand on my watch to see the time passing. I raised my hand to let him know when two minutes were up. He didn't earn any gummies for the first two days, so he wasn't very happy with mean old me. Day three was when things began to change. That day he earned two gummies. I gave him the treats behind the classroom door so the other kids wouldn't see the reward system. That same day, he took the bright red pencil that I had left for him and tried to print the letter D, the first letter of his name. His effort looked like an O but I was thrilled. It had taken me more than fifteen minutes before I could keep him focused long enough to do just that. I asked him, "Why do you like the red pencil?" "It's like Daddy's car," he replied. Gradually I lengthened the time between his appropriate behavior and receiving the treat. I also gave him an extra treat if he didn't yell at or hit classmates. I took satisfaction in knowing I had helped him to learn and to get along better with other little ones in his class. In return the little boy had taught me the "red pencil/red car" lesson—we sometimes value a thing not because of its intrinsic worth, but because we associate it with something, or someone, we love.

At the end of the placement I received a very high mark along with a supportive letter of recommendation from the teacher of these two students. These rewards were my equivalent of gummy bears—they encouraged me to believe I would be a good teacher.

After I graduated from Carleton I applied to the University of Ottawa's Faculty of Education. A few days after applications had been reviewed, candidates underwent interviews with members of the faculty. I was interviewed by the Dean. It lasted about three minutes (or so it seemed) and went like this:

"Hello, Ms. Jones. You have an impressive scholastic record. Congratulations!"

We talked briefly about my courses and my undergrad experiences. He told me a bit about Ottawa U., and then he cut to the chase.

"Ms. Jones, who is going to hire a teacher in a wheelchair?" he asked disapprovingly, "and how are you going to write on a blackboard?"

I was stupefied. I had no idea what to say and I had no instant or insightful thoughts about how I would be able to write on a blackboard or how I would convince anyone to hire me. I had learned in life to address challenges with forethought, and the man in front of me was allowing me none of it. His questions smacked more of predictions, even of accusations, than of attempts to understand my capabilities. I scooped my letter of recommendation off his desk, wheeled out of his office, tore up the letter and threw it in the garbage. I was furious because my practicum placement at the elementary school had proven to me that I could be an intuitive and insightful teacher. The Dean had destroyed that future for me.

So I simply left the University of Ottawa. I arranged a ride back to my aunt's house for the night and booked a next-day Greyhound bus ride to my parent's home.

I later discovered that what I went through with the Dean was in violation of the Human Rights Code, but I didn't know that at the time. In hindsight I should have pursued the matter, but during that interview my pent-up frustration at people in authority who rendered me insignificant overrode my tendency to act strategically.

It took me some time to decide that I should continue my education while working at the same time.

But I've had other, less formal opportunities to teach. Years later, I volunteered with a friend of mine to teach twelve year olds in a Brampton elementary school how to write poetry. We did this in weekly hour-long group sessions over several months. My friend and I were an excellent tag-team. In the first week of our effort we had very few participants and most were shy about trying to create even two lines of poetry. But when we turned the experience into a game, giving each child the chance to attach a poetry line to something ridiculous, funny, silly or naughty, more kids joined in. Once they had been enticed into putting their thoughts and feelings into poems, their poetry began to reflect the depth of their sometimes difficult life experiences. We the volunteer teachers became their trusted listeners. I still recall the pride in their faces when, at their "graduation" from the poetry classes, we handed each of them a book we had put together comprising the group's poems.

In 1985, while I was working as a March of Dimes Outreach Attendant Services Coordinator, I obtained a Human Services Management Certificate from Sheridan College by taking courses in the evening twice a week for two years. College was different from university: we were often asked to come up with problem solving ideas long before the professor even began to teach us something—a little like jumping into the pool before the swimming lessons began. I liked this approach. Those two years taught me how to develop practical cost-effective human service programs. Using this knowledge I later created a solid Outreach Attendant Services program for the March of Dimes that met the needs of people (including myself) and provided them with life-sustaining options they had never had before.

I've often reflected on my years of young adulthood—years of newfound friends and fresh experiences, but years too when my eagerness to learn was stymied by a skeptical driving instructor or a demoralizing dean of education. I've often wondered what I should have done differently. I've concluded that I had not yet developed the maturity or the knowledge about how to fight back. I simply walked away figuratively when people with power told me I couldn't do something, even when I knew I had the ability, if not the opportunity, to do those things.

When I was very young, my parents did the fighting on my behalf. As a young adult I hadn't yet figured out how to do it all for myself.

Years later I faced similar hurdles when I needed help to become a mother. This time I didn't walk away. I persuaded the skeptics that I could be a good mother. If I had not fought back, if I had simply left the room in anger and frustration, two wonderful women I'm proud to call my daughters would never have existed.

Had I learned to fight when I was twenty the same way I fought back when I was thirty, I might have become the superb teacher that I had dreamed I could become.

WANTING CHILDREN

After I learned that I wouldn't be accepted as a teacher in a wheelchair, I returned to Mississauga to live in my parents' house. I stayed with them for six months. Much as we tried to live together again, the experience was not very successful. My time in university had changed me. I was a different person—a familiar experience to anyone who left the nest and then returned. I no longer felt I needed to let anyone know everything I was doing or when I would be home. The natural protectiveness that my parents felt toward me, their little girl in a fragile chair in a big world, now felt confining, not comforting. I knew I could more easily define my life if I lived on my own and had a job.

So, armed with my education and fueled by hope, I became a volunteer and then a staff member with Ontario's March of Dimes.

In the eighties the Ontario March of Dimes was one of Canada's largest service providers for people with disabilities. I placed myself on their waiting list, hoping to eventually receive help from them with activities of daily living—things like bathing, grooming and getting dressed to face the world looking my best. I hoped it would be similar to the daily help I had received at Carleton University.

I went to my local March of Dimes office to tell their intake worker about my daily living needs. She told me I would need to wait for a while to get my needs met because in-home attendant services were only available to people who had been discharged from rehab hospitals and who agreed to live together in a group home. The thinking behind group living was that it allowed a small number of attendant service staff to serve quite a few people in one place. The intake worker said that Ontario's government was about to consider funding different service provision options. She said that while the March of Dimes didn't yet have the mandate or money to hire staff to provide different service options, it was recruiting volunteers to lay the groundwork for new services. She asked me if I would become a volunteer. I jumped (figuratively, not literally) at the chance to help create something new.

In the summer of 1984, I and two other ambulatory university graduates carried out this volunteer work, researching and determining, through telephone surveys of community service organizations and face-to-face focus groups with people with visible disabilities, what the needs were of people with disabilities who might be able to live independently.

After two months of volunteer work I applied for a job with Ontario March of Dimes. My job interview focused on how I could help them to articulate the challenges that people with disabilities would face if they lived independently, and whether I could generate "blue sky" ideas about other improvements—things like the integration of students with disabilities into mainstream public schools—that would make life better for people with disabilities. In April 1985 the Ontario March of Dimes hired me as their Outreach Attendant Services Coordinator. With only minimal Ministry expectations and guidelines, my job was to create an outreach attendant service model for the Region of Peel. The model would be a blueprint for helping people with physical disabilities in Mississauga and Brampton, including help with essential activities of daily living such as bathing, grooming, dressing, toileting, getting people positioned properly in their wheelchairs or other assistive devices and beds and helping with meal preparation and basic housekeeping. The model's services would have to be provided within the reasonable timeframes that able-bodied people would typically use to achieve these daily tasks. The model also had to be based on the principles of Independent Living.

Independent Living is a vision, a philosophy and a movement for persons with disabilities. Born on California university campuses in the 1970s, the movement spread to Canada in the 1980s, and has since reached around the globe and changed the way people view and respond to disability. It is founded on the right of people with disabilities to live with dignity in their chosen community, participate in all aspects of their life, and control and make decisions about their own lives.

The March of Dimes liked the model I designed. They asked me to develop a program based on the model and to recruit and supervise staff to provide the program's services in people's homes. At first I looked for attendant care staff who already had experience helping people with disabilities, but I soon discovered that some of the best staff were simply people who were passionate about helping others. I initially recruited and mentored ten staff to help twenty people with disabilities: we called them "consumers", hoping to avoid the dependency stereotypes that came with words like "clients". We were allowed to help each consumer for up to three hours a day. I developed all the policies, procedures and practices for the program and I established and maintained the program's details and support.

I and my staff learned much in the program's first year. We learned that people with disabilities can participate in many more ordinary life activities even when they get just minimal amounts of help. For instance, Mrs. A. was thrilled to be able to make a stew for her family once her attendant reached the ingredients for her and helped her to chop them up. A number of young people developed essential life skills like creating a budget and shopping for groceries, things they could now do with help from their attendants. The joy of going to a grocery store and making one's own choices about what to eat for a week was life changing for many people. Some of our consumers were happy because they no longer had to rely solely on family members for everything. Often my role became one of teaching consumers how to determine what their daily needs were, how to direct their own care and how to clearly convey their needs and expectations to their attendant. I also helped create a link with Peel Living, a subsidized housing provider. This link added a whole new supportive housing option for people in Peel with disabilities—people whose only previous options had been living with family or in an institution. The attendant service program's connection with Peel Living gave the program's consumers the chance to live in apartment buildings with access to attendant services at any time, day or night.

In June of 1985 I moved into a partially accessible apartment in Mississauga, a ten minute drive from my parents' home. Mom and I found the place just by deciding to take a drive one day, to see what apartments were available in central Mississauga. The unit I rented was bright and cheerful. I'm sure my parents were worried the day I moved out of the only home I had ever known, but they knew I had done well in university. Perhaps that gave them some comfort. By this time they had also accepted that I was determined to spread my wings. They knew I would leave despite their concerns. Once they accepted this, they went some distance to helping me turn my determination into self-directed living.

My apartment had low cupboards, counters, and sinks, as well as space under the counter so I could get my wheelchair arms partly under it (this meant I didn't need to lean perilously forward to reach the cupboards and use the counter tops). I could easily reach dishes and food packages and I could wash dishes and clean counters from a sitting position. It also had grab bars in the washroom and enough room in it to maneuver my wheelchair. Most of these features were new to me and gave me courage to attempt other physical tasks. Initially I furnished my place with old furniture and used items given to me by friends and family. I used plastic milk crates as storage bins and side tables, as I had done in my bedroom in Carleton University's residence. Once I had put a little money aside I bought things for beauty and pleasure. I learned that I had a flair for interior design, and I chose furniture and art work that created a welcoming home for my friends when they came to visit.

But I confess—from time to time I miss those milk crates.

I loved having my own home. It was comfortable and I embraced every aspect of controlling my own life. I loved sitting on my very own balcony, watching and listening to the children and teenagers in the playground and on the basketball court below my third floor apartment. Because a tenant in a wheelchair was a novelty to other tenants in the building, I attracted a fair amount of friendly attention. I struck up conversations with my new neighbors and sometimes I answered questions about disabilities that folks had not had a chance to ask before. It felt good to trundle my way through the lobby, met by the smiles and waves and greetings of others in the building. In particular I enjoyed watching the slightly fearful faces of young children break into smiles when they realized that I wasn't an alien, that I smiled and chatted and laughed and showed interest in them. I missed these little ones when I moved to my townhouse in 2006, but I met a new crop of kids to impress in my townhouse complex.

Once I moved into my apartment I became a consumer of the Outreach Attendant Services program that I had developed so that I too could have help in the mornings to get ready for work. Without that help it would have taken me four or five hours a day just to bathe and dress, followed by a full day of work.

There was an intimacy to the small program I had developed—an intimacy that sometimes felt good but that was sometimes painful. I and each attendant I had hired were very closely connected to the program's consumers and their families. When our consumers blossomed with new opportunities we were elated. When they suffered, we suffered. When a seventeen year old boy who was a quadriplegic died, his grief-stricken mother spoke with me daily over a long period of time, sharing her grief and searching with me for the meaning of her son's life and death. I had not yet developed a personal or professional ability to separate myself at times from the families, so I too grieved fully over the loss of this vibrant and fun-loving teenager. As time went on and other consumers died, I recognized how deeply I was affected by these deaths. Near the end of that working period I learned that I still wanted to help people, but I needed to work—at least for a while—in an environment that didn't always put me in direct contact with clients who were struggling to live.

In 1998 I left my March of Dimes job to move on to another challenging position.

It was also in that decade that I began to understand that I was unlikely to get married. Most of my interactions with men by then had highlighted fears on their part that they would have to look after me if we connected for the long term. I grew to accept the single life and I decided that I would not define marriage as a yardstick for success or failure in my life. I was able to separate the rite of marriage from the importance of a loving relationship in my life (something I will always want).

While I got comfortable with this probability, I remember feeling sad for my dad: despite my acceptance of this probable reality, I would have liked it if he could have wheeled me proudly down the aisle of a church someday.

After accepting the single life, I became increasingly aware of my desire to have children.

I never once thought that having a child would be a way of ensuring life-long care for me, even though I have been told that others, rather unkindly, saw this as a reason why I chose to have children. Rather, I wanted people in my life that I could love fiercely and take care of through their growing years and forever. While I was contemplating this idea, I came across a newspaper article that described a group called Single Mothers by Choice. I attended close to a year's worth of monthly meetings of that group because these women wanted exactly what I wanted. Most participants lived in or near Toronto. Several offered their houses for meetings and suggested topics for discussion. Using Toronto's Wheel-Trans and sometimes friends for transportation, I went to every meeting as long as it was probable that I could enter the house where the meeting was held. A few times, access barriers kept me from attending.

The group members were liberal and open minded women, but the fact that I might become a mom in a wheelchair was incomprehensible to most of them. I could often sense this, based on their looks of hesitancy when I came into the meeting in my wheelchair. I imagined them thinking, "How is she going to safely lift and move her baby while she is in that chair?" Some women worked up enough gumption to ask me direct questions. "Are you sure you can even get pregnant and have a baby? How are you going to be able to take care of the baby?"

I did my best to answer them with kindness and respect: living with a disability usually involves explaining oneself to others. Questions from able-bodied folks can be seen as intrusions, or as opportunities to teach. I prefer teaching—I must have been a schoolmarm in an earlier life.

I attended the meetings to learn how to undergo anonymous donor insemination or in vitro fertilization and how to deal with family reactions to this choice. Several women in the group were embarking on this process for the second or third time, so they had experience dealing with family reactions. They shared their stories with me. To this day I feel a profound sympathy and kinship with the women I met in the group, particularly women who gave so much of their time and energy, and exposed themselves to indignities and condescension from an unsympathetic world, only to fail in their attempts to conceive.

I also approached several male friends in my life to ask them if they would consider being live donors for me. Two of them said they would, but I learned that if they did, they would have equal parental rights by law. Since I knew I would not have a traditional relationship with them, I decided that would not be a wise choice for me. The man with whom I have now had a long-term, long-distance relationship was at that time willing to have a child with me, but his much earlier vasectomy could not be reversed and he eventually said: "OK, if it's not me, maybe it should be the turkey baster." Thus I embarked on the process of anonymous donor insemination (ADI).

Most of the women in the Single Mothers by Choice group were connected to a fertility clinic in downtown Toronto. Since I wasn't aware of any similar clinic where I lived, I connected with that well-known one.

The process required me to get to downtown Toronto by 7:00 a.m. every month for three mornings in a row following a menstrual cycle. During these mornings the fertility clinic conducted blood tests and vaginal ultrasounds to test for optimal fertility times. For most women who attended this insanely early clinic (insane for me, given the transportation arrangements I had to make), the process took ten minutes. But my veins are tiny and giving blood samples was an ordeal. After a couple of months my arms looked like the arms of a drug user.

Each of my visits took at least forty minutes. Friends then drove me to work by 9:00 a.m. I did my best to appear normal and unstressed at work on each of these mornings. The clinic would call me back in the afternoon and tell me to return later that day if I was ready to be inseminated. Other parts of the ADI process included a financial assessment, a session with a psychologist and an in-depth medical examination. I underwent all of those components and passed them without incident.

In the summer of 1991, Toronto General Hospital called me and asked me to attend a meeting. The hospital was affiliated with the fertility clinic that I had attended, and the hospital's medical staff were responsible for starting and overseeing the ADI patient processes. My partner and I went to the meeting together.

We entered the meeting room, and I found myself face-to face with ten doctors. Initially I was not overly anxious, even though I assumed that I would yet again need to convince people that I would be a good mother.

One woman in the room did appear very anxious. She asked me to confirm that I had gone through the initial steps and that I had passed every one of them. She reminded me that the financial assessment had been done to confirm that as a single mom I would have enough income to support a child. She also reminded me that my meeting with a psychologist had been held to ensure that I could mentally and emotionally cope with the realities of being a single parent. I said that I had gone through each step and that from my perspective everything had been successful.

Then, a bombshell. "Ms. Jones, we have decided that we are not going to inseminate you. We once inseminated a woman with multiple sclerosis and she ended up dropping her baby."

For a few seconds I could think of nothing to say. I trembled. I wanted the floor to swallow me up. My journey to become a mother seemed to be over. My loved one grabbed my hand under the table and said, "Say something, Lisa". Without moving, I whispered, "I don't know what to say." But after a few more seconds, I said, "Do you know the difference between MS and cerebral palsy? MS is a degenerative condition. Cerebral palsy, which is what I have, is not degenerative. If you don't know the difference between these two major causes of disability, you're in no position to know what I can and cannot do. I will make sure that I don't drop my child."

Far too often, people with disabilities face similar interactions with "experts"—with well-meaning people in authority who see a disability as something that prohibits normal life, people who say "No you can't" rather than "How can I help you work around this challenge?"

Some of the experts in that meeting (who typically hadn't bothered to introduce themselves) tried to justify the decision of the medical group. But I couldn't process what they said. I said to my partner, "Let's go." We left the room.

Once we left the hospital my tears started. I said: "Honey, let's go back to the fertility clinic. The head doctor there may be able to help me". So we went back to his office. The doctor's daughter, who was the clinic's office manager, saw me and said: "My dad has left the office. He won't be back for a while". We sat in the waiting area. Four hours later, the doctor returned to the office. "Why are you here? What happened?" he said.

I filled him in on what had taken place.

"I expected you might face that," he said.

"OK, what do I do now?" I asked.

He said, "Write me a paper. One that describes in detail how you will look after your child from birth until the teenage years."

I replied, "Sure, I'll do that and send it to you. If I write it, will you do the inseminations that I need?"

"Yes", he said.

"Am I writing this paper to cover your butt?" I asked.

"Yes" he replied, with a reassuring smile.

We drove back to my house. With help from my partner I wrote a detailed document in an hour. In it I said I would hire a live-in nanny to help me with some aspects of physically caring for my baby. I said I would use a power wheelchair instead of a manual one so that I could safely transport my child around, and that by doing so my baby and I could engage in activities together. I said I would get help to design a specially adapted crib so I could safely transfer my little one into and out of it—knowing that my father, a professional draftsman, would be part of my "design team". I said that when my child started school I would volunteer in my child's kindergarten class so children in early grades could see a mom in a wheelchair and perceive her as someone normal. I said I would figure out how to use my reduced physical capacity in ways that would allow me to lift or move my child.

True to what I had written, I achieved all these things.

The insemination process was simple. The sperm was injected into me and I lay still for a while so the sperm could reach the fallopian tubes where conception happens. The process was very clinical and not at all romantic, but it was very much tied to hope that a wonderful baby would come my way. It discouraged me when my menstrual period recurred: it meant I had to go through the process all over again.

Four months passed. One afternoon in October of 1991 I got a phone call at work from the fertility clinic's nurse.

"Lisa, you're expecting!" she said.

After a pause to try to absorb the news I said, "What? Say it again please."

The nurse repeated the good news, then she laughed, saying "Yes, you really are expecting."

I thanked her, hung up the phone, and closed my office door for a few minutes so I could absorb the news that I had been afraid I would never hear. I stifled a desire to shout with joy.

During the whole process I had confided in a few close friends at work. It was now time to share my news with them and to ask them to become part of my baby's life and future.

I went to the office beside mine. I said to my colleague, "Guess, what? I'm pregnant. Would you like to be my child's godfather?"

After he said "No way!" we started laughing and he said "Yes, Lisa, yes I will."

I asked another co-worker to be the godmother. She also said "yes" immediately.

A week later, it was Halloween night. I decided that would be a good night to tell my parents because they would have to keep it together enough to deal with the trick-or-treaters arriving at their door. Until then I hadn't told them about my plan to have a child because I thought they wouldn't see motherhood as something I could embrace because of my disability. I believed that they wouldn't see me as physically capable of caring for children. Even though they had seen my capacities develop over the years and had helped me to build those capacities, they also carried in their hearts and minds that deeply ingrained parental need to protect their child. I thought they might feel compelled to protect me from my own decision.

When I told them, they were both visibly shaken and pale. Women in the Single Mother's by Choice group had warned me that many parents react this way when a grown single daughter announces a pregnancy. Then, a barrage of questions and comments: "Who told you to do this? Were you raped? You can't always have what you want, you know. You can't even tie your own shoelaces, how are you going to do up the child's shoes? Who is the father?"

I remained calm. I said, "I will work out the details, and since I'm 29, I don't have to ask for your permission."

While I was not seeking permission, I was very much hoping for understanding and support—if not right away, then before my child was born. Ultimately both my parents showed the love and the strength of character that I had expected of them. Now that my own children are grown, I recognize in myself the same urge to protect and to shelter my not-so-little ones just as my mother and father had tried to do when I ventured into a broader world than they had envisaged for me.

EARLY YEARS AS A MOTHER

My Beautiful Girls

My first pregnancy was initially uneventful. In the beginning I made regular visits to a traditional obstetrician-gynecologist. She and other medical, nursing, and diagnostic staff in her office and at Credit Valley Hospital in Mississauga were non-judgmental and supportive. None of them questioned my motive or my capacity in giving birth and raising a child. I followed the usual prenatal routine: taking prenatal vitamins and visiting my doctor regularly. I didn't do anything different from what any other woman would do.

Then things turned. Three months into my pregnancy I developed an abscess near the anus, a condition often mistaken for hemorrhoids, which is what I assumed I had. I was finding it very uncomfortable to sit in my chair. I begin to feel signs of general infection, including fevers and nighttime chills.

I took a couple of days off work thinking I had the flu, but when my fever reached 104 degrees I called my family doctor. She admitted me to hospital immediately.

The surgeon who examined me asked me to consent to surgery to remove the abscess. He told me it was possible that neither I nor my baby would survive the surgery. When I signed the consent forms I told the surgeon, "If you have to choose who to save during the surgery save my baby and give her to my mom." I knew my mom would care for the baby, even though she didn't fully understand or support my choice at the time. I knew that once my baby was born my mom would fall in love with the little one at first sight.

After surgery I spent a month in the hospital recovering. I was given strong intravenous antibiotics and pain medications to counteract two liters of poison in my body. Shortly after I first received these meds I could no longer feel my baby moving inside me. My obstetrician told me the baby was just sleeping because of the drugs I was taking. She said it was not customary to do ultrasounds on fetuses three months of age and older, but in my drug-induced state and because of my own poor health at the time, I was afraid my baby had died. I begged my obstetrician for at least one more ultrasound to show me that the baby was alive and well. She agreed, and the ultrasound proved to me that my precious baby was fine. I could finally let myself rest and recover. Five months later, two weeks ahead of the ninth month, I went back to the hospital to deliver my beautiful baby.

A friend from work had offered to be my birthing support person during this time. I gratefully accepted her offer. She helped me to get ready for my hospital visit, she bought gifts for me and my baby and she helped me deal with the process and discomfort of having the epidural put in my spine. The anesthesiologist responsible for the epidural found it hard to get the needle into my not-so-straight back and said, "Can't I just put you right to sleep? It will be much easier than doing this." I said "No, I want to be awake when my baby comes out." So he persevered and ultimately succeeded.

I had a planned caesarian section. During my hospital stay a major challenge I faced was getting the hospital to allow my attendant to come to the hospital to help me during my time there, both before and after giving birth. Once I had my daughter I had to stay in the hospital for one week due to a sudden bladder infection. Two days after her birth I desperately needed to shower, but the nurses were too busy to help me with it. I explained to the hospital's Director of Care that the nurses were too busy to provide me with the help I needed to complete my usual morning activities such as showering and changing my clothes. The Director was responsible for ensuring that nothing happened to my attendant or to me while on hospital property, but she understood why I needed to get out of bed and bond with my girl. She admitted that due to time constraints the nurses couldn't help me with my daily routines. I agreed to assume full responsibility if something happened to my attendant or me and nothing ever did. After that, the hospital allowed my attendant to help me for an hour or so each morning.

My beautiful daughter, Laural Victoria Rhiannon Jones, was born on June 30, 1992 at 9:30 a.m. Long before she was born I had read a lot about baby names. I learned that in the ancient world a green crown or wreath of fragrant laurel leaves was given to the winners of contests and battles. Laurel wreaths adorned the images of kings and emperors. The name Laurel sounded beautiful and full of meaning. My cousin suggested changing the spelling to Laural so my baby would not be associated with Stan Laurel of the Laurel and Hardy comedy team. I was fine with that suggestion. Victoria is the female version of my paternal grandfather's name Victor, and Rhiannon—a name famous in Welsh folklore—was a beautiful and unusual name, and the title of one my favorite Fleetwood Mac songs.

My mom, my aunt and my grandmother (Mom's mom) came to see Laural later that day.

My mom became fully supportive and helpful in many concrete ways shortly after I had my daughter, although she initially worried that I would drop the baby. She became a typical grandma eager to cradle her granddaughter in her arms. She later pampered her with cookies and field trips to get ice cream or to buy things at the toy store.

My dad came to the hospital the following night. He brought me chocolate bars and asked me, "Where's the baby?" When the nurse came in with my daughter, my dad took her in his arms and kissed her. He never saw me watching him, but I knew from that moment on he would love her unconditionally.

Within our family and circle of friends, Laural is known affectionately as Lou—a nickname given to her by my aunt, who called her Laural Lee Lou when she was just a baby. The Lou part stuck. To me it will always be more than a nickname. It is the token of a bond between Lou and the people who still call her by that name—people I love dearly. My dad had called her Boo Boo, and Lou decided at an early age to call him Papa.

Dad and I designed an accessible crib that had one side that opened like a door. Since he is a draftsman by profession, he drafted blueprints to guide him in making it. I gave blueprints to others who were interested, and the crib design was given to the Centre for Independent Living (CILT) Parenting with a Disability Network (PDN).

I have since been able to share those blueprints with others and I later gave my crib to another mother in a wheelchair. For my own use, I also designed and used an apron-like contraption, sewn for me by my aunt, which I draped over my head and down my body. Then I attached it to the baby with Velcro straps so that I could wheel myself and the baby around while also ensuring Laural's safety.

I also had a wide tray created that also attached to the arms of my wheelchair with Velcro straps. When I covered the tray with soft pillows and baby blankets, Laural would lie snuggled next to me in her little nest to relax and sleep, even while I was moving from place to place in our apartment.

I had already chosen a nanny to help Laural and me. A friend knew a woman who had come from Jamaica to get Canadian citizenship and to work as a nanny for another family, but the family had suddenly moved away. I hired her as a live-in nanny just weeks before Laural was born. Initially it was challenging for us to connect, because she came from a different culture. This meant that she sometimes handled babies differently than I. As a gesture of love and caring she tended to feed Laural more frequently than I knew was necessary, but eventually we worked together to establish and maintain a normal and reasonable feeding schedule that made me comfortable. I had learned in a life filled with helpers that negotiating task details works better than peremptory orders: our nanny had a generous heart and an understanding nature, so we were able to smooth out issues like feeding fairly easily. Our differences melted away and we became close (not hard to accomplish in my two-bedroom apartment).

I confess that in the early phase of my motherhood, I was sometimes jealous of her simply because she could do some things for Laural that I could not, but in the face of her sure-handed gentleness with my little bundle and my own increasing self-confidence as a mother, jealousy soon faded. I developed a strong appreciation for her help, her kindness and her amazing spicy jerk chicken. I also saw, more intimately than ever before, the grit that lies within Caribbean motherhood. Her own son was still in Jamaica: she had chosen to leave him there with family while she ventured into a new cold country, fueled by the dream of bringing him to Canada someday. On occasion I was lucky enough to learn about her anchors here—her church and the many kindred-spirited women in that church that enveloped each other in love and concern.

She lived with us for a year and a half until my daughter was walking, making it easier for me to manage child care tasks, so she moved on to another job. Shortly after, her own son—still in Jamaica—was diagnosed with leukemia. Her family members and friends raised money so her son could be brought to Ontario to receive the treatment he needed, which was not available in Jamaica. Despite those loving efforts he did not survive.

When she died in 2015 I attended her funeral with at least a hundred other mourners. I met many of the people she had helped through her church life. Whatever Canada had given her, she had given back a hundredfold.

I had always wanted to have two children, in large part because I believe a child should have at least one sibling if possible—someone to share with, someone else to cherish throughout life. It's not right for everyone, but I know it was right for me and my children. I was able to use more of the same frozen sperm that I saved in the sperm bank I used to conceive Laural. This means that both sisters are completely biologically related. After one miscarriage and six years later, I felt that I was being supported by God and that He absolutely trusted me as a mother!

Emily Grace Bronwyn Jones was born on August 13, 1998. Em was also born by caesarian section. I gave her names I had chosen and loved even before Laural was born. I knew I couldn't easily give Laural six names so I put the others aside for the child I knew had yet to come. Getting Mom and Dad to accept my second girl was much easier than before. Quite far into the second pregnancy, my dad saw that I was getting bigger. He called and said, "Are you expecting again?" I simply said "Yes" and that was the beginning and end of those questions. Once again I was supported and assisted during my pregnancy by another woman I worked with who also became the godmother to my girls.

I had expected that little Em would not be a carbon copy of her sister. How right I was, and how happy I was to see Em's own wonderfully independent spirit emerge even when she was tiny. It also heartened me to see how quickly Lou loved and nurtured her sister, and how quickly Em responded with affection, bordering on adulation, toward her big sister. The two remain almost mystically connected to each other even to this day.

When Emily became part of our little family I hired two women, each part time, who took turns staying overnight, helping me with feeding and diaper changing. I felt that I had more independence and autonomy when I hired those part-time overnight employees to help out rather than depending on live-in help, even though the nanny that we had when Laural was a baby was a wonderful woman. And by the time Em was born I had greater confidence in my own competence.

What did I encounter and what did I learn as a young mother?

Most broadly, I learned that there is no such thing as love with a disability. There is merely, and wonderfully, love. On wheels or on foot, it works its miracles.

Now the specifics.

I learned that parenting provides an opportunity to teach children how to make a difference in the world and how to capitalize on their talents and skills. Parenting with a disability means that you have to be creative and more patient than other parents. You need to be adaptable and willing to give up some physical tasks and activities by letting someone else do them to ensure the well-being and safety of your baby. When I took my girls to play-and-learn programs such as swimming, for instance, there were things I couldn't do, like taking them into the water, so I asked the swimming instructors to help out. They were very receptive and took my kids into the pool for me so I could watch them learn to swim.

I hope my ability to adapt and to improvise, and the importance of allowing others to be your helpers, have set a good example for my daughters. They both show every evidence of deep wells of adaptability. Both have a rich history of helping and being helped by others. These virtues come almost entirely from them, not from me, but I believe I at least gave them initial fertile ground for their growth.

When my girls were in kindergarten I volunteered in their classrooms. The other kids got used to being around me and accepted my disability. My kids didn't seem to be embarrassed about having a mother with a disability, but when they were preschoolers, each of them thought I should learn to walk or that a doctor should fix my legs. I tried to truthfully answer their questions such as, "Do you think if you try hard you can walk soon, like I can? It's not too hard, Mom, just go like this…"

They may have thought about what it would be like to have a mother without a disability, but if they did, they didn't tell me about it. I know they wished that I could skate and roller blade with them, but by and large I was just a single parent mom with an amazing wheelchair that they could use by either by sitting in it or on my lap or by standing on the back of it to get rides to and from school.

The biggest barrier I faced as a parent with a disability was and still is acceptance by the general public that people with disabilities can be good parents. The biggest attitudinal barriers came from people who would say things like, "Single women with a disability shouldn't have children" or "You only want children so they can look after you" or "You must be a lesbian because you chose to have children the way that you did." Friends have told me they've also heard people say, "Maybe she was raped" or "The Children's Aid will take away her children, at the taxpayers' expense."

Sometimes these comments are wrapped in a supposed concern for the wellbeing of children. This makes the barbs all the more hypocritical: if you are worried about my ability to be a good parent, then take the time to find out what I've done to make sure I'm a good parent. Find out what I can do rather then what I can't do. My personable, competent and accomplished daughters are proof of my capacity to raise children.

And I think I speak for all parents with disabilities when I say that we feel no obligation to justify our choices and competencies to every Joe or Jill on the street who think they have a right to judge us. I am always ready to answer well-meant questions. I am never ready to be backed into a judgmental corner by people who believe I am guilty/ incompetent until proven innocent/competent.

One interesting outcome of my parenting as a mother with a disability has to do with a "can't" and my adaptation to that limitation. I could never physically coerce my children into doing what they needed to do. What I could do, however, is use calm explanation to help them understand, even at a very young age, what they should do and not do. This meant I also had to patiently listen to their side of the story and negotiate compromises that still protected them. We talked a lot, we argued a bit. I'm proud to say the both my daughters are excellent conversationalists and debaters, skilled at interpreting their own case to others when need be. They both developed a lawyer-like talent for making their case in arguments, but they also developed the negotiator's knack of knowing when to accept a good compromise.

When Laural was about five years old, she needed brief hospitalization to deal with an infection. The hospitalization entailed the inevitable needle—something Laural was desperate to avoid. But rather than trying to kick and scream her way out of the needle, she marshaled all the arguments a five year old could come up with to persuade the adults looming over her bed not to give her the needle. She didn't succeed, but even as the needle entered her arm she was still desperately elaborating her argument. I was proud of her that day; I am proud of both of them, every day.

Em and I, it turns out, are remarkably similar in how we solve problems. I call it "solving by stewing". As someone with a disability I need to think my actions through carefully, to minimize the chances of screwing up. So I sometimes think a problem through, visibly and with some anguish, before I finally decide what to do. It can alarm people around me who mistake my thought process for panic. Em is similar, although she has no disability. She thinks carefully, investing emotion as well as logic in how she decides. But when she does decide, she commits herself fully to the results of her decision. The people she loves are better for it.

My parenting choices aren't right for everyone. Each person is different. You need to know how you will make your child safe and how to help them to feel secure, and you need to become comfortable with your own particular parenting style. Developing this comfort level is often a challenge for a parent with a disability, simply because other folks have doubted your competence. Parenting with a disability means that you have to be creative and more patient than other parents. You need to be adaptable and willing to give up some physical tasks and activities by letting someone else do them to ensure the well-being of your baby.

As a parent, you need to realize that you can't protect your children from many of the challenges that kids face, whether or not their parents have a disability. Both my children, for instance, were bullied because they had a mother with a disability, but kids get bullied for all sorts of reasons—being too tall, wearing different clothes, using a wheelchair. The judgment of whether or not a child should be created in the first place should not rest on whether they might be bullied at some point.

When I was planning my pregnancies and raising my daughters, few published resources existed to help me. But since then, the Centre for Independent Living, Toronto (CILT) has published three books drawing on my experiences and the experiences of fellow single parents, to help other parents with disabilities:

- *The Parenting Book for Persons with a Disability: From planning your family to raising adolescents*
- *Nurturing Assistance: A Guide to Providing Physical Assistance for Parents with Disabilities*
- *School Year Chronicles: A Personal Collection of Your Child's School Year Memories, Including Tips and Resources for Parents With Disabilities.*

BEYOND MY OWN MOTHERHOOD

Sometimes book-learning, valuable though it is, isn't enough. I and several other mothers with disabilities helped to create a peer support and information-sharing network for parents and prospective parents with a disability that runs with support from the Centre for Independent Living, Toronto

For three months in 2004 I was seconded from my planning job at the Peel-Halton District Health Council to the Centre for Independent Living, in Toronto, to help the staff establish a direct funding program that would allow people with disabilities to hire their own attendants to help them. The program required that selected participants with disabilities could become managers and could also learn about employment standards requirements and other obligatory government expectations related to hiring, retaining, firing and paying staff. I created and prepared the initial fundamental policies and procedures for that program.

Another area of interest and need was developing a Parenting with a Disability Network for people with disabilities who were parents or were considering parenthood. My role in helping to create the Network lay in meeting with individual parents and parents-to-be, to get a sense of what they wanted to gain from a network and what they could offer through the network to other parents. Most people I met with were mothers or women contemplating motherhood. Other service agencies showed little interest in the creation of the Network, but CILT persevered, creating the Network to connect new parents with disabilities with veteran parents, who helped them cope with challenges they would encounter.

By the end of my three month secondment the design of the Network had been completed, but dissemination of information about the Network to prospective members had only just begun. Several of the women who had confided their hopes and anxieties to me kept in touch with me by phone so I could provide them with advice and a friendly shoulder to lean on until the Network was up and running.

What I heard and learned from these women lent credence to my own experiences in journeying to motherhood, but what these women taught me transcended my own experiences.

I learned that the road to our motherhood passes by flashing neon signs that say CAN'T and SHOULDN'T, signs put beside the roadway by people who love us dearly and people entrusted with the job of helping rather than hindering. Our own families—people who have loved us, cared for us, protected us, strengthened us for all our lives—sometimes balk at the notion that we could become parents. They worry for our sake. They worry for the sake of our children yet unborn. In this nexus of love and protection lies an irony. Once we become parents ourselves we feel the same protective urge toward our children that our parents felt toward us. And sometimes we don't trust our children's ability to choose for themselves, for fear there is undue risk attached.

There is another wonderful irony in our families' concerns. The very love that leads them to protect us and discourage us from parenthood can lead them to nourish us and our children once we become parents. My own parents, despite their initial fears, became wonderful grandparents, proud and eager to empower my children. Of course, being parents they second guess me from time to time, but they do it from love.

But at the time a person with a disability has decided to be a parent, their own parents' fears can be overpowering. I had a conversation with a woman and her live-in boyfriend who were ecstatic to learn that they were expectant parents, until the woman's parents punctured their bubble of joy. Although their daughter was independent and gainfully employed, they felt her moderate cerebral palsy rendered her physically incapable of the responsibilities of motherhood. Their joy turned into conflict and anxiety.

I've learned that helping professionals—doctors, lawyers, accountants, and the like—are often skeptical when they encounter or advise a person with a disability who wants to have a child. Trained in minimizing risks both to their clients and themselves, they are at times reluctant to embrace the mission of helping us to achieve our dreams, opting instead for advising us to abandon the dreams. One of the virtues of a network of parents with disabilities is the sharing of information about professionals who are sensitive to our dreams and willing to help us.

I've learned that we with disabilities have our own well-grounded anxieties about our ability to parent well—anxieties that often center on pragmatic issues like holding, moving, feeding and protecting babies and toddlers. Parents with disabilities need support from other people with disabilities who can affirm that they're going to be able to do a good job. I had the honor and joy of doing that for some folks. I was also able to share information about the techniques and strategies I developed to be able move my children around safely. I've shared with others the blueprints of the crib that my dad modified for me so I could wheel right up to and under the crib, then open a door-like railing to get my daughters out safely into my lap.

I learned that fundamental distinctions among disabilities need to be recognized and acknowledged. For example, a mother unable to get out of bed, an employed mother with a visual impairment, and a mother with an intellectual disability might be grouped together and compared with non-disabled mothers. Each disability requires its own sensitivities and its own adaptations.

Parents with disabilities are not saintly parents raising saintly children. As parents we are as prone to make mistakes as anyone else, and our children are as vulnerable to difficulties and wrong choices as any other child. Yet I have learned too that when disabled parents have troubled children, it is often presumed that the parents' disability caused the problem, without considering any other contextual factors. Poverty, parents' history of abuse as children, family disintegration, substance abuse, lack of adequate support—all can create challenges utterly unrelated to disability.

MY BEST VOLUNTEER EXPERIENCES

Throughout my life I've been a volunteer, partly to meet new people, partly to hone newly acquired skills and partly to help people. But an undercurrent in my volunteer work has been a desire to let the world know that a woman with a disability can contribute fully to the improvement of her community. Too often the world sees people with disabilities as takers, not as givers. Too often people with disabilities are not encouraged or allowed to exhibit their caring skills as volunteers for fear of liability issues, or for fear that a volunteer with a disability would drain away staff resources in helping the volunteer.

Since I expected that at least some of my volunteer work would involve public speaking I joined the Mississauga club of Toastmasters International to improve my speaking skills.

I've served as a volunteer at my children's elementary schools, tutor for the Peel Literacy Guild, vice-chair of the board of Mississauga Community Legal Services, co-founder of the Parenting with a Disability Network, chairperson of Peel's Transhelp Advisory Committee, chairperson of the Peel Attendant Services Advisory Committee, member of the Ontario March of Dimes Provincial Attendant Service Committee, member of the Peel United Way Allocations Committee, member of the United Way Citizens Review Panel and a big sister serving with Big Sisters of Peel.

All these experiences were interesting and rewarding but two in particular gave me immense satisfaction and pleasure. They taught me that I am most fulfilled when I help others.

The first was my volunteer work with the Peel Literacy Guild. Through the Guild I taught a young father how to read. He and his wife had a little boy, a bit over two years old. The father's goal was to learn to read at least one story to his son.

During my first meeting with the father he explained that he and his brother had been raised by their grandmother. His brother had an intellectual disability and had attended special education classes. The grandmother wanted the brothers to stay together, so she sent my adult student to the same school as his brother. He told me that when you are placed in an environment where only minimal learning and comprehension is expected, that's all you will achieve.

He asked me (as many people do), "What happened to you? Did you have an accident?" I told him I used a wheelchair because I had lived with a disability since my birth. I told him a bit about my own life experiences, to let him know that we were both people who needed to transcend the expectations that others had of us.

In the second part of our first conversation my student said, "Are you embarrassed to be with me because I can't read?"

I replied, "Are you embarrassed to let me help you learn to read, because I have a disability?"

We both smiled at each other and each said "No."

The Guild's volunteer training taught us strategies to improve literacy, but I relied just as much on my intuition and instincts. I spread all the letters of the alphabet on the floor and asked him to tell me the names and sounds of each letter. The first time he tried to do it he made an intense effort, but he needed help. I then asked him to mix up the letters on the floor and put them back in the proper order. We started singing together: "A, B, C, D, E, F, G…"

I then taught him what letters in combination sounded like. For example, the letters "a" and "r" together sound like "are" so if you put a "b" in front of those you get bar. Then there is tar, car, far. The next week when we met I said, "Here's a word you can teach your son. It is far plus a 't'. Very confidently he began to sound out that word. Suddenly, he stopped. I said (knowing full well) "what's up?" He said: "I don't think I need to teach him the word 'fart'—he'll figure it out!" We laughed and I said, "OK". My student progressed very well.

Thus began his journey learning how to read. Within two weeks he knew the sounds of all the letters. He began sounding out simple words.

One of my challenges was helping him to decide what would be a fitting story for him to learn to read to his son. He didn't want to stay in the program for long because he wanted to go away with his wife for their anniversary in eight weeks. We had only two months to meet his goal.

Five weeks into our time together I thought of a book that he might want to read to his son—Robert Munsch's 1986 book *Love You Forever*. I owned a copy and I had already read it to children I had babysat.

I asked him if he liked the story's message about the eternal nature of a parent's love. He said "yes", so for our last three weeks we read the story together at the end of each literacy lesson.

A few weeks after he and his wife returned from their anniversary trip, he invited me to their home for lunch. I met his wife and his little boy. His wife confided to me that in the past week her husband had been reading the *Love You Forever* book over and over to their son, much to the little boy's delight.

But it wasn't the only book he was now confident enough to read. As their toddler was tucked in for his afternoon nap, I heard his dad in the background, appraising the value of green eggs and ham.

I left their house with a smile on my face.

My second deeply rewarding volunteer experience began in 1989. I was twenty-seven and thinking about having children, but I still had planning to do before that could happen. I decided to learn more about children by becoming a volunteer big sister through Big Sisters of Peel.

I completed the mandatory training and passed the criminal reference check.

Initially, new volunteers took part in large group activities with girls ranging in age from six years to the early teens. My first few big group events didn't connect me with a girl in need of me as a role model. I was worried because I didn't drive and all volunteers were supposed to be able to pick up the girl to whom they would be matched. I thought, "I'm gonna go through this whole process and in the end not be matched with someone because I won't be able to pick her up and bring her home after our time together." Still, I thought I couldn't just give up on this opportunity. So I talked to the Director of the organization. I said to her, "When I get matched with a child, would you allow my mom or my dad (who had agreed to do this) to be the ones who will pick up my little sister and bring her back to her house when our visit is over for the day?" She said, "I can't promise anything but I'll see what I can do."

Two weeks later, at a group event, a little six year old girl was introduced to me. Immediately this beautiful girl climbed onto the footrests of my wheelchair and threw her arms around my neck. I returned the hug immediately and said "Hello—it's nice to meet you, little lady. How are you?"

One of the staff people told me the girl's mom had agreed to let my parents be her daughter's chauffeurs. I was so happy!

The next day my parents drove her to my apartment. Our first visit involved a TV movie and a big bag of popcorn. The little girl told me that she really loved her mom. She said she had a brother. She also told me that she would be seven years old in a week, so we talked about what kind of cake she wanted for her birthday. Even though we were warned against spending too much money on our little sisters, I gave in to the temptation to give her an inexpensive little gift every time we were together, which happened once a week and sometimes twice.

She was a weekly part of my life for four years.

Our times together included a lot of movies, something we both enjoyed. We saw *Home Alone*, *Toy Story*, *Mrs. Doubtfire*, *The Santa Clause*, *Babe*, *Flubber* and *The*

Borrowers to name a few. We went shopping and Halloween trick or treating. We went on picnics and enjoyed planning the picnic menu in advance. I helped her with homework and we went to arts and crafts events hosted by Big Sisters of Peel. We even went bowling, but I confess I wasn't very good at it.

I sometimes felt badly because I couldn't join her in her baseball and volleyball games, but she didn't seem to mind. We often went to my parents' house to swim in their pool and to have dinner with them.

My little sister was chatty, full of curiosity and eager to learn. In my kitchen she learned to bake cookies and muffins. I was the grateful beneficiary of her new culinary skill.

I attended her first communion at her family's Roman Catholic church along with her mom and her brother. Her mom and I both took part in getting her ready for this very important event. She was a little over seven years old at the time. She looked beautiful on that special day!

She trusted me. She didn't care that my way of moving around was different from hers. Long before my children came along, she could be seen hitching a ride on the back of my wheelchair so we could get to our chosen destination quickly. She was my special guest at my brother's wedding in June 1992, a few days before my first daughter was born.

In my family photo and memory book I keep a letter from my little sister, telling me how happy she was to meet my daughter, and that the baby was beautiful.

After the birth of my daughter it got harder for me to see my little sister on a weekly basis, so after a time we only saw each other occasionally. When she became a typical young teen she preferred to hang out with her friends. But our early connection enriched and strengthened both our lives.

On the surface my friendships with a man who couldn't read and a little girl struggling to grow under difficult circumstances were one-sided: I was the giver, they were the takers. But my experiences as a literacy teacher and as a big sister immeasurably enriched my own life and helped me to determine what I could excel at.

Teaching literacy to a man with unique learning requirements helped me to understand that just as each learner is different, each teaching technique must adjust to the needs and aspirations of each learner. Through initial conversations with him I learned how deeply he was motivated by a desire to read stories to his son, and I found a method that taught him how to read rather quickly and that left him with strategies and approaches he could use forever to read new stuff. And he left me with a sense that I had what it takes to become a teacher.

My time with my little sister from Big Sisters of Peel was also a learning experience for both of us. Our connection gave my little sister the opportunity to be spoiled just a little and to have some attention paid directly to her on a regular basis.

At that time her mother had challenges in life that made it hard for her to focus on her daughter. But I could focus on that little girl, without usurping her mother's love, and I loved doing it. With my gentle encouragement she developed the courage to try new things, and like a good big sister I cheerfully ate all the things that she learned to bake no matter how they turned out (fortunately they usually turned out well). With her, I learned when it was necessary to set parameters, when it was necessary to accept her choices and when it was necessary for us to make a joint decision. From me, I believe that she experienced unconditional love and consistent encouragement, and she developed a sense that more in life is possible than others expect of us. She bore witness to this when she discovered that I was going to be a mother despite my wheelchair—or more accurately, despite what others thought a woman in a wheelchair could and should do.

As I helped my own children to grow I used some of the ways of teaching and supporting that I had developed through my connection with my little sister and my Literacy Guild student.

MY AMAZING HUMAN CONNECTIONS

No life worth living is lived in solitude. What follows are my tributes to some of the friends who became extensions of my family—people who mean much to me—and some of the events I've gone through with them. Many friends have been omitted, not because they are any less important to me, but because I wanted to give you a representative sample of those folks who have become part of me, just as I have become part of them.

But first, a word about privacy. Because I have a visible disability the world doesn't always afford me the privacy that people need and deserve. As a result, privacy is something I respect highly. In writing this book I thought long and hard about how to respect the privacy of the beloved people I write about.

I came across an on-line article by an author grappling with this same issue who decided to write about people, and how she connected with them, without naming them. Her decision makes ethical sense to me and seems preferable to using fake names. My exception to this rule—I use the names of my brother Steve, my accomplished and beautiful daughters Laural and Emily, and my doctor Lori Coman-Wood, with their permission.

I am drawn to people who know who they are, individuals who are not focused on characteristics such as appearance, since physical attributes will change. The people who light fires in my soul are all passionate about something. They have led me to re-invent myself on an ongoing basis. They care about me and they respect me. They have changed who I am.

My People of Faith

In my teens I developed an interest in exploring religions. I shared my interest with a co-worker and her husband, and the three of us attended a Baptist church together every Sunday for more than a year. It was there that I first discovered how quickly and deeply I am attracted to voices. The minister at that church mesmerized me with every sermon. I paid attention to the sermon's messages and took them to heart, but I swear if that man had read a telephone book one Sunday, I could have easily recalled a huge percentage of the phone numbers he had read. After a year he moved to a different church too far away for me to hear his sermons each week, but I kept in touch. On separate occasions he baptized my two daughters at my parents' house. I recall with warmth and gratitude how easily he embraced the arrival of my girls, baptized them and simply asked me to provide them with a strong and loving foundation upon which to grow. Beneath his warm voice lay a warm soul, ready to embrace anyone.

I'm a sucker for good voices. The man with whom I have a long-term, distance relationship also has an amazing voice. It's one of many reasons why I'm connected to him. I've told him that he should been a late-night radio talk-show host, based on a voice that flows like melted chocolate, I'm compelled to listen to whatever that voice wants to say.

Since my connection with the Baptist minister, I've maintained a desire to learn about the purpose of humanity in the world, and how religions express that purpose. A man I worked with, a practicing believer in the Baha'i faith, gave me many insights into our spiritual purposes. From the time I first met him I admired how he stayed calm, grounded and caring to all those around him under circumstances that would have driven me to anger. I wanted to understand why those virtues seemed rooted in his DNA. I wanted to project the same quiet confidence that he does. I discovered that his confidence was driven by a strong conviction that the world is basically good—a conviction drawn from his Baha'i faith. I learned that a fundamental aspect of this faith is the need to unify humanity.

I and a fellow worker listened to his gentle descriptions of his faith. Aware of our growing interest, he asked us if we wanted him to lead regular sessions with us after working hours, so we could better understand Baha'I faith. We readily agreed.

Abdu'l Baha, the founder of the Baha'i faith, said we must consider all God's servants— meaning all humanity—as our own family and relations. He asked us to direct our whole efforts toward the happiness of those who are despondent, to give food to the hungry, to clothe the needy, to glorify the humble, to help every fellow creature. By doing these things, he said, we attain the good pleasure of God. I now try to meet these expectations every day. I try to disregard shallow and divisive differences among people. I try to understand their deeper commonalities. Reducing that shallow level of observation means I can focus more on what people do to create and live their own lives in connection to the lives of others. I can more readily appreciate each person's unique choices and contributions.

Perhaps I would have come to understand these spiritual truths merely by reading Baha'I scriptures, or by reading the scriptures of one of the many other faiths that bring light to darkness. But I had the privilege of meeting a man whose daily life bears witness to the scriptures of the faith he readily shared with me and others.

A Friend, a Family, a Tree

I keep a letter tucked in my memory book that had a huge impact on how I try to connect with people. The letter is from the mother of a woman friend of mine who died in 2006 from the effects of alcoholism.

Tall and reedy with a shock of tousled hair, my friend turned men's heads, but she could be loud and opinionated in public, and lost friends and lovers because of it.

I first met her when I was in my twenties. She was seven years older than me. One day, close to Christmas, I went into a salon to have a manicure. She was one of the nail technicians. As I wheeled up to her cubicle she said, "Pull up a seat and sit over there. I'll be with you in about ten minutes." The comment evoked a gasp from other customers who had seen me enter. I could tell what they were thinking: did that woman not see the girl is in a wheelchair? After the ten minutes I went back to her station and I could see that she was laughing under her breath. I understood what was so funny! During my manicure, we engaged in small talk and at the end of my visit she said, "Hey, I'm having a Christmas party at Mom and Dad's next week. Would you like to come?" Even though I wouldn't normally go to the home of someone I had just met, I said "Sure."

The next week I rang the doorbell of her parents' house. An older bulldoggish man—her father—looked at me from the doorway. Next I heard, in a gruff Scottish voice, "Hey girl, did you invite someone in a wheelchair? You better get her in then." Thus began a long friendship with her and with her parents—a gentle English-born mother, and a Scottish father who was a retired Toronto policeman.

She and I used to hang out with each other at least once a week.

One evening we decided to go to a bar, a gathering place she often visited. On the way there in her car she suddenly exclaimed, "Oh shit, there are about twenty steps to get into this place, and I forgot all about your wheelchair. How are we gonna get you in there?" We decided fate would find a way, and in the end we asked the bouncer to help. He carried me up like I was a feather. He sat me on the top step and simply pulled my chair up.

On this occasion and many times thereafter, she forgot about my wheelchair. She saw the person, not the hardware. Like many others in my life, she made it easier for me to be spontaneous in a world in which I normally had to plot each activity with care. And she could make me laugh.

But her often biting sense of humor disguised a troubled life and a string of relationships with men that ended badly.

She told me about her struggles with alcohol. I attended a number of AA meetings with her.

I also began to understand that her relationship with her father was troubled. Kind-hearted though he was at his core, his disapproval of his daughter's way of living her life dominated their relationship.

Her mother and father became an important part of my life, my partner's life, and the lives of my children. We often visited them at their home in the countryside an hour east of Toronto, greeted on each occasion by mountains of good food, rides for my daughters on their lawn tractor, and on one occasion the gift of a hand-crafted doll house, a beautiful and precise piece of workmanship that must have taken hundreds of winter hours to build.

My friend eventually moved to Calgary and pursued a successful career as an insurance investigator (a good fit for her no-nonsense personality). A few years later, in 2006, she died unexpectedly, the result of her addiction to alcohol. Yet she still lives in my soul. She still makes me laugh. I still cherish her.

After she died I received this letter from her mother:

My dear Lisa,

When I received your package last week, I read the letter and then the children's book you sent me: "Guess How Much I Love You".

Then I read your letter twice and three times, absorbing your message.

I realized that you as my daughter's friend accepted her as she was without criticism. That is something we as a family did not do. Unfortunately her father was very critical of her as a child. I do not think he was meaning to be cruel, but he hoped she would succeed where he had failed. They were great pals though, going camping and fishing until my Mother came between them, and things were never the same.

I had my own objections to her way of life too but as she grew older, mine was more a sadness as she missed out on so many things.

I feel we were all were outside of many of her inner feelings. We will never know now.

Our love to you and your family at the end of this horrible year. Let's hope 2007 is better. Bless you.

Mum & Dad

Before she left Ontario my friend bought her own small jewelry shop. In the shop window she had placed a potted fig tree, an elegant bush whose will to survive in that north-facing window matched the will to survive of its owner. When she sold the shop, she gave me the tree (we had named him Benjamin). I put Benjamin in the sunniest corner of my apartment's living room. His leaves half concealed my little ones when they played hide and seek. One year he was recruited as our Christmas tree and spent a month clad in shimmering silver. Benjamin died as unexpectedly as my friend had, but while he was alive he reminded me of her every day. Like her, he reached for the sun.

And I still think of her every day, even without Benjamin to remind me.

I remember the moment when, reflecting on her untimely death, I said to myself, "Life can be short, I need to make sure that everyone I care about knows for sure how much I love and care about them, so I don't ever have to worry about what I didn't do or say once I can't change my actions." This was what Oprah Winfrey calls an "aha moment". I made a choice to tell family and friends, on every possible occasion, what they mean to me, and that I love them.

I am tied to a group of good friends who share my values—a non-judgmental respect for other people, an acknowledgment that our individual lives are not fully lived until we reach out to help others, and a recognition that to achieve our individual complete personhoods we must re-inform and re-invent ourselves as often as we need to.

I know from experience that these values are not achieved simply or easily. But I also know from experience that they are more easily achieved with the help and love of those we allow into our inner lives.

From Childhood to Forever

Two close friends are women who have been cherished parts of my life since childhood. We've shared much together over the years. Our families were neighbors, we played and laughed and cried together as children, and as adults we supported each other as we raised our kids. These women have both readily and regularly provided gifts to help make my life a little easier now that I'm no longer working.

My friendship with them teaches me that matters of the heart endure and strengthen. Matters of the mundane and immediate, along with matters of the intellect alone, can lose their relevance except in memory, and matters of the purely physical wind their inevitable way down after a time. But the heart and the people in it, properly tended, live on.

My Working Sisters

Others in my circle of friends are warm people-focused women I met through my work life.

The first woman, tall and with the air of an athlete to her, is someone to whom the terms "distinguished" and "elegant" would apply.

I met her when we both served on an advisory committee for specialized public transit in Peel Region. At that time she was the executive director of an organization in Peel that provided support to people with multiple sclerosis (MS), a disease that has its own special cruelty to it: people with MS may experience symptom-free periods that give them hope of recovery, to be followed by crashes into full-blown recurrence of their debilitating symptoms. So my soon-to-be friend had plenty of experience with the psychological devastation and demoralization that disability can produce.

I have known able-bodied people—good folks indeed—who provide service to people with disabilities and who develop a protective shell as a result of their work. They serve the best they can, but the shell prevents them from developing friendships with people with disabilities that are based on equality or depth.

But my "MS friend" hadn't developed that shell.

When I entered the room where our first committee meeting was about to start, she said "Hi" and then a look of surprise showed on her face. It was evident to her that I was pregnant. After the meeting I told her that I was going to have a baby soon. She asked me a few questions—kind rather than skeptical questions—about how I would take care of my baby while in a wheelchair. Since this was my second pregnancy, I shared with her how I had taken care of Laural and how I had used the help of the live-in nanny that had been with us. She was impressed with how I had worked out the details of being a parent to my first daughter. She remained supportive and interested in how things would go with Emily. I was touched by her interest and her warmly expressed belief that I was a great mom.

We soon stopped being work colleagues, but we became close friends. She came to my baby shower held to celebrate Emily just before she was born. She has remained connected, and because she has become a world traveler since her retirement, I'm always eager to hear the details of her latest overseas adventures. She in turn remains interested in what are often mundane details of my life and the lives of my daughters. She has a rare ability to display genuine interest in even the smallest shared details of a friend's life, salted when necessary by an irreverent sense of humor that relishes the ironies and absurdities of life. For two decades now we have connected over coffee and restaurant meals as often as we can.

In 2018, my friend shared with me that when we met, it was the first time she had ever seen a pregnant woman in a wheelchair!

The second woman was a consultant I worked with in Toronto for Metrolinx, the Greater Toronto Area's leading public transportation authority. Together and in partnership with my Baha'i friend, we staffed an inter-agency committee helping to find ways to remove barriers that affect people with disabilities who have no other choice but to use specialized transit. Based on specialized transit rules in place at that time, people with disabilities could not use anything other than the specialized transit services available in their geographic area. That meant that a disabled person who lived in Mississauga could not simply decide to go to Oakville to visit friends via transfer to Oakville's specialized transit unless he was also been declared eligible for the specialized services available in Oakville. The process of confirming eligibility for someone already eligible in another system was complex and drawn out.

Together she and I were an excellent team. Given our different work and life experiences we could examine the project's challenges from several different sides.

She and I understood many of the difficulties associated with making changes in large bureaucracies, but our heart-driven focus for that project was finding ways to get people with disabilities wherever they wanted to go, without first requiring them to overcome bureaucratic barriers and limitations. We were able to uncover the depths of fear and frustration that many people with disabilities face when they have to use a service that doesn't respond to some of their key needs.

I admired her ability to get committee members to consider new ideas. By asking them to clearly articulate their worries and concerns, she would come back to the next meeting with several proposed solutions that were rooted in the committee members' own lived experiences. She was also a consummate sleuth, ferreting out solutions that worked in other communities and presenting them to the committee.

Our committee's work resulted in a memorandum of understanding endorsed by all specialized transit providers in the Greater Toronto Area (GTA)—an amazing outcome of our efforts. It meant for example that someone who was a registered specialized transit User in Oakville would be guaranteed a required ride by Peel

Transhelp and could go anywhere in Mississauga without having to re-apply for the service.

I daresay our friendship was forged in the same way that soldiers who win a battle together develop a camaraderie that includes but transcends their time together in the trenches.

Before and after committee meetings she and I would chat. She told me about a volunteer French club she was part of. She asked me if I wanted to participate and I said yes. I spoke French well during my university years, but I've lost a lot of that ability since then. I learned from her that her father had been a renowned chef who had served many famous people, including the King of Sweden. As a result, one common topic of interest became our desire to discuss, create and share good food.

She is a giver. Helping an elderly friend is something she does regularly, transporting her to the supermarket and helping her with her grocery shopping every week.

Whenever I get an email, text message or phone call from her, she begins it with "Hello, your Gorgeousness!" I sometimes wonder if she has forgotten what I look like lately.

Newcomers Become Friends

Two sisters from India that I know are women who have shown me what immense courage newcomers to Canada can bring, and what results their bravery can produce. I initially worked with one of these women and later met her sister. Through my conversations with them I now understand how cultures submerge women's identities, rendering them submissive but not invisible: they weave their own sisterhoods of blood or friendship to nurture each other.

The sisters determined that they couldn't become the people they wanted to be in India, so they moved to Canada. I admire their determination to learn things about themselves and to become the individuals they feel they should be. I also admire these two women for their easy acceptance of me and others. When I worked with one of them, I recall being surprised that she never asked me why I used a wheelchair. She exhibited a quiet acceptance that together we had to come up with new transportation options to meet the needs of people who have intellectual and cognitive disabilities rather than physical ones. Based on this silent but strong respect that we maintained for each other, our joint work efforts were rewarding and successful. Our work enabled both of us to develop a deeper respect for people with intellectual and cognitive disabilities, people whose societies (here and in India and everywhere) have traditionally shunned and ridiculed them.

Helpers Who Became Friends

Two other valued friends are women who first connected to me because they provided me with attendant services at home. One of these wonderful women still helps me out in the morning. She has been doing this for me for close to sixteen years. The other friend assisted me for many years, but because she has a daughter with a health issue, she had to make changes in her life so she could concentrate on meeting the needs of her daughter. Our friendship has deepened over the years, and like my university roommates, she has become a non-biological sister to me. We try to see each other every weekend and I've spent a lot time with her immediate family. While her special-needs daughter and I cannot communicate in a traditional way, we share a rich and calm sentiment of love, coupled with unspoken understanding and caring when we are together. That young woman, though she can't speak, calms me when I am in her presence. She has been a gift to me, and I have tried to be a gift to her.

Another important and cherished woman in my life is my doctor. She listens, she responds, she respects, and she cares. She gives me clear information and she explains the impacts of a range of treatment options. She recognizes that I am the only person who lives in my body and the only person who will determine what works best for me. I often ask her for information or clarification about what other medical people are doing to me. She expresses her pride in my parenting styles and she values the intuitive insightful and helpful nature of my daughters.

She is also my friend. She recently told me that she is actually part of my family—to that I say, absolutely!

The Godfather

The man I asked to be godfather to my girls is someone I began working with in 1988. He is warm, caring, and insightful. He often expresses how well I've acted as a mother. Since he still has a highly demanding work life we don't get to share time together often enough, but we talk as often as possible and get ready to share our next dinner. He is a talented writer and musician, and I hope he sees a shadow of his own writing and lyrical talents when he reads this book.

My Four Musketeers

In 2012 I decided to leave my unfulfilling job take a two year contract position helping to improve access to public transit for people with disabilities in the Greater

Toronto. The new work was very demanding but I enjoyed it and I did it well. When my contract was not renewed I was devastated and initially angry at myself for giving up a full-time job (albeit an unfulfilling job). I had no way of predicting the gift that would be given to me following the end of the contract—the gift of enduring friendship.

I am tied to my four former co-workers that I view now as brothers. For five years now, almost every month since the contract ended, the five of us (or most of us) get together over lunch to share what we're doing. We also talk one-on-one between lunches.

One of these men easily makes me laugh. He always provides information on surveys or studies that he has heard about that interest the rest of us and he uncovers interesting facts that lead to intense conversations among us. Since he has young daughters, we like to hear about their new and exciting experiences.

The next man is a movie buff. We often discuss new or old movies that have affected us. I also love movies in traditional movie theatres, where the experience includes a big bag of popcorn (to which I acknowledge an addiction) and a soft drink.

My third friend is kind to everyone. He is detail-oriented and works hard to leave a small footprint on the planet. He will do almost anything for anybody. If he doesn't know how to help someone he researches the possibilities until he comes up with a solution that will meet that person's needs. Like me, he has a sweet tooth.

The fourth man is Italian by heritage, making him the most comfortable of all with receiving and returning a hug along with a kiss on each cheek. Like the others, meeting the needs of someone who needs help is paramount to him. When we have lunch he tells me regularly that his Italian DNA requires him to pick up something for anyone of us to eat or drink.

My Friend, My Cabbie

A friend for the past thirty years, the driver of an accessible cab, has been a quiet advocate, hero and voice for people with disabilities. Many of us have had to deal with cab drivers who would rather not deal with what they consider the hassle of serving people with disabilities: we are seen as burdens, not as customers. They reflect this in sullen or rude behavior when called upon to serve us. But my cabbie friend uses his vehicle as a tool to ensure individual dignity and inclusion. He has done much to help his passengers, many of whom have become his friends, to participate in life's experiences, without feeling they are seen as a burden to the taxi industry. People with disabilities make it to school, work or social events because of the hundreds of rides he provides every month. People living in long-term care facilities make it home to their families for Christmas because he works for many hours on that day. He has picked up and taken home people with dead wheelchair batteries when no other options are available. This man still hopes that the public transportation system will improve to provide better timely and equal service for all. He works every day to move this goal forward. On top of this, he is a talented and sensitive songwriter and musician.

But helping others as constantly as he does, imposes its own burden on him. Exhausted and dispirited on occasion, he needs people who give to him from time to time, not merely take. I try to be one of those people.

A Friend Who Makes Beautiful Things

Another friend played a huge part in helping me to have my second daughter. I met her when I was a guest speaker at a conference about mothers with disabilities. She was at the conference serving as an attendant, providing personal assistance to participants.

Laural, four years old at the time, attended the event with me and joined me on stage as I spoke. Part way through my presentation boredom overtook her. She bent down in front of me and removed my left shoe. My audience chuckled. I smiled and I kept on speaking. The attendant who became my friend quietly approached the stage, put my shoe back on my foot, and found a cookie for Laural. I was touched by the gentle and respectful help she gave others that day. At the end of the conference I asked her for her business card, knowing I might need her help as an attendant at some point.

She had grown up in rural Northern Ontario in a Jehovah's Witness family that did not encourage higher education, deeming it unnecessary for the pursuit of paradise on earth. Despite that, she gathered up enough courage to go to community college although she had been told that God might strike her down for doing so. She moved to Mississauga and became a superb designer and craftsperson in wood, creating furniture that melded the functional with the beautiful. She accepted commissions and exhibited her work in public shows.

Two storage chests, which I called memory boxes, were crafted by her for my children. They attested to her creativity and skill, and to the love she gave to both girls—but to call them "storage chests" doesn't do them justice. Each chest blended different kinds of wood into a harmonious clean-lined whole. They are identical, except that each girl's full name is carved into the lid of her box—Laural Victoria Rhiannon Jones and Emily Grace Bronwyn Jones.

She provided me with occasional attendant services over a two year period, but more importantly we became friends. She accompanied me to many fertility clinic appointments in Toronto during my efforts to conceive a sibling for Laural. We often shared lunch and confidences before she drove me home. Given her upbringing, I could only imagine some of the initial thoughts that she might have had to consider, contemplate and maybe even suppress when she learned that I was already a mom in a wheelchair who was also deciding to have another baby when she entered my life

After Emily's birth and my return to work, my friend was Em's babysitter for a period of time. Several times she took Em to meet her Northern Ontario family. I'm told Emily won their hearts.

My friend has an adventurous side to her, a trait she shared with my wonderful rule-breaking daughter Laural. I recall my friend's motorcycle, a roaring monstrosity to me, but something she tamed well enough to take Laural for careful bike rides in the nearby deserted GO train parking lot on weekends. Laural, clutching my friend tightly and grinning with pride, loved the adventure.

By her example she helped both my girls to learn to transcend conventional gender roles, to bring flair and creative joy to whatever they do. I daresay she taught me too, and I think our enduring friendship is predicated in part on a shared belief that in our lives we must rise above what people expect of us.

The Man I Love

Yes, I'm in love. I've loved the same man for thirty years and he loves me back. We are not married to each other and we live some distance away from each other, yet we connect emotionally, mentally, intimately. I'm aware that I'm fully embraced by the man I love. I know without question that he would never choose to love somebody simply because they can walk—or because they couldn't walk.

Our relationship is not traditional and its richness lies beyond my capacity to describe, but then none of us will ever be able to explain what someone means to us, traditional or non-traditional. People on the outside will see us for what they think we are. But none of that compares to what you feel with the one you love. It is here, connected with the person you care about, that you can create your own rules, expectations, and definitions of love. Navigating the vast expanse of different relationships is terrifying—there are no predetermined rules and infinite chances to screw up. But it's in this sometimes perfect, sometimes miserable space that we learn what our wants, needs, and expectations are, through trial and error. We learn what it takes to make us happy.

When we first met, he noticed my chair for about the first ten minutes. After that it disappeared. Obviously, he deals with it when we are together, but to him it's akin to the fact that I have brown eyes: it helps describe me but it doesn't determine me.

When we first met, I noticed his smooth gentle voice for the first ten minutes and for the thirty years thereafter.

While his love for me is not influenced by my wheelchair, he has a depth of understanding of how disability affects my life. As he once wrote to me:

> *"How could you not wonder whether life would have been better if you didn't have a disability? Most of the universe tells you that you are a lesser being (although a small part of the universe grants you uncomfortably heroic status). Those who love you know differently, but that is scant consolation for how the rest of the universe sees you. And at the level of hour-by-hour practicalities, you live in a world that is more difficult for you to manipulate than it is for me. But I also know that Providence gave you a fierce intelligence, a profoundly deep heart, and the stubbornness to tell the dark part of the world to go fuck itself. I believe your task is to nurture those three assets within yourself.*
>
> *And all of this only has meaning if you invest it with meaning. You know that I believe part of that meaning for you might involve you bearing witness to your life in both words and actions, talking back to the universe, responding to what the universe has erroneously, unfeelingly, and sometimes with wanton or neglectful cruelty, told you that it believes about you.*
>
> *Many of them want to suggest an immediate 'fix'—something they see as easing life for you, but that you see as assaults on both your dignity and your capability. Some of their misguided advice to you is rooted in love and in a desire to ease you pain. But some of it is judgmental under-estimation of your astounding capacities."*

I confess to an initial curiosity about why he would pursue a relationship with me, rather than with an able-bodied woman. My curiosity, initially tinged with skepticism, came in part from my previous experience with a dating website. One man responded to my profile by letting me know he liked what he read about me, but the fact that I used a wheelchair was a non-starter for him.

To the man I love, the answer to my curiosity was simple. My disability, he said, is one characteristic out of the many characteristics that comprise me and my life. To him, accepting the totality of who I am includes accepting my disability, not as a drawback to be tolerated, not as a defect to be ignored or euphemized, but simply as part of who I am. Case closed, from his point of view.

Thoughts on Friendship

There is a dark undercurrent in some people's thinking when it comes to people with disabilities and their able-bodied friends. I've seldom directly encountered this undercurrent, but friends have told me about it.

The undercurrent has several parts to it:

- A belief that the relationship between an able-bodied person and someone with a disability is exploitive. Either the able-bodied person is the exploiter ("Why else would she have a gimp for a friend?") or the person with a disability is the exploiter ("She's probably just using the friendship to get free help.")
- A belief that friendship between a person with a disability and an able-bodied person is fundamentally unequal: one person in the relationship exhibits dependence, and the other exhibits pity.
- A sense that the able-bodied friend deserves congratulations and admiration for condescending to hang out with a person with a disability. The friend with a disability, on the other hand, should be grateful that a "normal" person is willing to be her friend.
- A belief that a person with a disability is most comfortable with friends "of her own kind" ("After all, they would have so much in common, wouldn't they?") This version of the undercurrent assumes that ones' friendship with others is shaped largely by only one factor: one's visible ability level.

I don't know that many able-bodied people hold these stereotypes, but even a few is too many. So in case any of the readers of this book hold to those stereotypes, let me be clear. My friendships are all two-way. I give as much as I get in each friendship. I look upon my friends with great gratitude, and they look upon me with gratitude too.

I'm currently not working. As a result, people in my highly treasured group of friends have chosen to trust me to help them when they face life challenges. I've been told that I help reinstate calmness and clear thinking, and provide hope for people who feel like they have lost those attributes. It's my honor to help friends when they need me.

The reader may have noticed that with one exception, the friends I've described are people without what one might commonly call a disability. I've certainly had friends with disabilities, and at one time I had a brief romantic involvement with a lawyer who used a wheelchair. But my "friend pool" is broader than that.

But like many people with disabilities, I have at times benefited a great deal from friendship with people who face the same kinds of challenges that I do. I understand that for people with some kinds of disabilities—hearing disabilities for instance—problems of communication with most of the rest of the world have led to the growth of strong, enduring, and nurturing disability-specific cultures.

I feel a special kinship with folks with profound deafness. Just as I faced society's expectation that I would want to learn to walk, however awkwardly, deaf people have faced the expectation that they should want to learn to lip read and to communicate with their voices, rather than learning and using the rich, deep form of communication embedded in American Sign Language (a language I have striven to learn, simply because it's beautiful).

MY HOUSE, OUR HOME

In 2004 I realized I had to find a new place to live for myself and my two girls. We had lived in two separate apartments in the same apartment building in central Mississauga. Both apartments had been easy to access and they were partially adapted for people who use mobility devices. But in 2004 a resident in our apartment building was killed by drug dealers, so many tenants left the building. I became increasingly concerned about the safety of my children. I began to think about possibilities.

Because of the reorganization of the district heath council system where I worked from 1988 until 2005, I had been assured that my severance package would be large enough to let me make a reasonable down payment on a place to live. I wanted the extra space a house would offer, I wanted a patch of outdoor greenery to call my own, and I wanted the freedom to adapt my living space in ways that were only possible through ownership rather than rental.

But it would have to be a house suitable for a woman in a wheelchair. It actually took me close to two and half years from the time I started looking in 2004 until I found a suitable and modifiable location.

I began searching with help from a real estate agent whose daughter had a disability, but unlike me she could walk. My parents, who had a lot more experience than I in terms of owning homes, also helped with the search. We looked at a few houses that had already been adapted for wheelchair users—there weren't a lot of these on the market, even fewer were in my price range, and almost none had been adapted in ways that met my needs, so I decided to buy a townhouse and have it adapted from scratch to meet my needs. Townhouses tend to be less expensive than freestanding houses, in part because they're constructed on a smaller plot of land. But being on smaller lots, they maximize the use of the lot by being multistory buildings rather than bungalows. So a two story townhouse it would be, even though bungalows are friendlier for people who use wheelchairs.

Initially my real estate agent and a physiotherapist suggested that I could use a stair lift chair to get me upstairs once I knew where we were going to live. That idea didn't sit well with me (excuse the pun). I knew that once I reached the top of the stairs I would have to get off the stair lift chair and transfer back into a wheelchair that would always have to be located upstairs. I could envisage myself falling down the stairs while trying to get into the wheelchair.

An elevator would be the only practical and safe solution. The front foyer area of a house would be the best location for an elevator, but safety laws required that there be enough room beside an elevator to allow walking people to use the stairs.

Once I located a suitable house we found a way to install an elevator from the ground floor to the second floor. I also wanted to use it to access the basement, but that would have cost an extra $10,000. I didn't have the money to do that. So our basement has been *terra incognita* to me. I've never been there. I'm not about to shinny down the stairs to the basement on my backside the way I did in our home when I was a child. I've relied on cell phone photos, and the accounts of intrepid cellar explorers, to tell me what goes on down there. The basement is primarily a storage space, a laundry room, and a den (with couch, bed, and washroom) for my daughters and their friends.

The three of us moved into our townhouse in October 2006. By then Laural was busily making new friends in high school. Em, who had been fearful of moving to a new location where she knew no one, soon began to bring to our home newfound friends from the street to meet me.

In 2017 I applied to the Region of Peel's Home Renovates Program and I was the first person whose projects were accepted in that year. With this funding I hired contractors to install cameras in my basement that transmit their images to my cell phone, and I was also provided with an emergency back-up generator.

The coolest thing that I possess now is my generator. It means I won't be stuck in the house in case of power failure or fire. The elevator, lights, microwave, and garage door will still work.

The house has three bedrooms on the second floor. Two of them were for my girls. The third—the master bedroom—was large enough to allow us to accommodate my elevator and to create a separate accessible washroom with a deep tub for me in about a quarter of the bedroom's space (there was already a bathroom for the girls on the second floor and one in the basement). The remaining bedroom spaces are snug but practical.

Like most houses, ours has several stairs from ground level to the front door. An external wheelchair ramp would have been a possibility, but the condo association didn't want condo owners to change the look of the exteriors of their houses. I also knew that an outside ramp would ice up in winter, so my dad came up with the idea of installing the ramp inside the one-car garage, from the garage floor to the door between the garage and the main floor hallway. It's an ideal solution, leaving plenty of room for garden tools and my manual wheelchair in the rest of the garage. I enter and exit the house through the garage door. So do most of my walking friends.

The back of the house has patio doors opening onto a small back yard and beyond that, a paved tree-lined walking trail through the townhouse complex, frequented by dog-walkers and neighbors out for a stroll. I love sunshine and hot weather, so six years after we moved into our home, I asked my dad to me build a backyard deck. He designed it and built it so well that he could have made a tidy sum from building similar decks for neighbors who saw and admired his handiwork. I spend a lot of time on the deck in the summer, moving from time to time to get out of tree shade and back into full sunlight. The deck has a dining table, large flower pots, and nearby a bird-loving Saskatoon berry bush where birds and various other creatures keep us amused with their chirping and posturing for much of the year. But being my father's daughter and abhorring a mess, Saskatoon berries that fall from the bush onto the deck in the fall, and that get squished into purple jelly by my wheelchair wheels, drive me nuts.

Whether I'm on the back deck or outside the front door beside a little café table, I spend many a summer evening getting to know my passing neighbors. I take particular joy in new kids in the neighborhood who see my wheelchair first, and only thereafter see that there's a human in the chair—a lady who loves to engage them in teasing conversation.

A couple of years ago I gave a ride in my power wheelchair to a little guy I had come to know who lived across the street. After the boy's mother called him to come in the house for his nap, a man approached me, introducing himself as a neighbor who lived in the condo next to the little boy's family. I had seen him around before, but we hadn't spoken.

He told me he enjoyed hearing the little boy giggling during his first power wheelchair ride. I said I had enjoyed it too. I learned that my neighbor, who was in his forties, lived in his condo with his parents so he could help them out as they grew older. I learned that his father was from England, like my own father. He told me his mother, in her late seventies, was still working. Beginning from these sparse commonalities, we chatted often thereafter on warm summer days, sitting at the café table outside my front door. I enjoyed his affable gentleness and his spirit of caring about his family and about the neighbors around us. We became friends.

If you meet him you can't help noticing that he is largely covered in tattoos. This took me aback a bit when I met him: I belong to a generation that sees something a tad dangerous, something of a foolish whim, something of an outlaw, in well-tattooed people. Instead I met a man of great sympathies, a man whose decisions—including decisions about what tattoos to get—were never foolish whims. When asked, he would describe the origin of each tattoo and its significance. I learned that tattoos are an aesthetic extension of the big-hearted principles by which he lives his life.

Here we were on summer days: a woman defined most visibly by her wheelchair, a man defined most visibly by his tattoos. Both of us prone, perhaps, to shallow judgment by others, both of us much more than we appear to be in the eyes of others.

I still sometimes share brownies and ginger ale with my tattooed friend with a heart of gold.

Some neighbors, in all innocence, express surprise when they meet a single woman with a disability with two children and who owns her own home. I use these moments of surprise to do some gentle and friendly teaching about disabilities. Many of these neighbors have never had a conversation with a person in a wheelchair before. I try to make their first such conversation a pleasant and enlightening one.

But In our house, one of our friends is not human. After much cajoling from my daughter Em, I finally consented to the addition of a cat as our housemate. This may not seem like a big deal, but I had no previous experience with pets. I'm afraid of horses, dogs make me nervous, and I worry about cats getting caught under my wheels. But our cat Meeko is a lovely little guy, skilled at avoiding my wheels, utterly devoted to Em, and demonstrably fond of my mom and dad when they visit.

Me, he usually tolerates and sometimes loves.

I've told you so much about my house because it's a big part of my life. It's something I'm proud of. And I think you might be interested in the factors that a person with a disability must take into account when she buys and lives independently in a house.

But as I describe our home, I'm very much aware that many people with disabilities aren't able to achieve this level of housing independence. Many will never be able to get jobs that let them accumulate enough capital to invest in a house. Many will live in solo or shared rent-geared-to-income apartments, or with their parents, or in plain little rooms in facilities meant to house people with disabilities.

I may have been luckier than them, but I'm not better than them.

All of us, with or without disabilities, want to live in environments over which we have some control. But control over one's environment is difficult for many people with disabilities, sometimes for financial reasons and sometimes because a world that considers itself benevolent enough to provide us with housing also considers itself qualified to decide what that housing would look like: our job as people with disabilities is merely to appear grateful.

So, dear reader, if you ever have a chance to support government policies and practices that allow people with disabilities to exercise greater control over their environments—policies such as guaranteed annual incomes or disability pensions (called the Ontario Disability Support Program in Ontario) that don't claw back the gains and assets that some people acquired before needing disability pensions. We can do better than the philosophy of requiring people to strip themselves of their assets, to reduce themselves to destitution, before they receive our help.

When I've attended conferences and other gatherings of people who use wheelchairs, I'm interested by how creatively some folks accessorize and decorate their wheelchairs. Personalized storage bags, stickers with slogans on them, scrollwork on the metal parts akin to tattoos, flags flying from miniature flagpoles attached to seat frames—all of these are ways people with disabilities express their individuality and their control over an environment they inhabit for much of each day—their wheelchairs.

MY RANT

As we go through life, disabled or not, things happen that bother us. It could be something someone said to us, the way someone acted toward us, or the way someone made us feel.

I'm an optimist. I'm pretty good about letting things go and moving on. But I simply can't easily let go of a few things that have bothered me, no matter how hard I try.

So this is the part of the book where I feel sorry for myself—something generally considered a tedious character flaw. But a friend once told me that feeling sorry for oneself from time to time is normal and a good idea as long as one moves beyond the sorry state fairly quickly. I think he was right.

So here goes!

It frustrates me when people see physical disability as anything other than a life reality that requires me to be creative to find ways to address the reality. The challenges I encounter in my daily life don't define my motivations, my ambitions or my identity, so why do some people have preconceptions about what cerebral palsy (or any other disability) means to me or anyone else? Perhaps it should not surprise me but it still does.

I've had a few demeaning interactions with people when I've sought help from our society's helping, systems, particularly the health care system. A couple of examples:

When Laural was almost five years old I became pregnant for a second time. On our way home from her weekly dance class I knew something was wrong. When we got in our door I said, as calmly as I could, "Honey, I have to ask one of our neighbors to stay with you for a while. Please dial 911 on the phone and press the speaker button." Since she loved pressing buttons she complied. Shortly after that an ambulance came and I was taken to the hospital. A friend in our apartment building stayed with Laural, gave her a snack, and tucked her into bed.

When I got to the hospital the ER doctor confirmed what I suspected. I was having a miscarriage. As I was being examined and a nurse was being told what had to happen, the doctor said to me, "Are you sure you can be a mother given your disability?" As this question was coming out of the doctor's mouth, a lot of blood was coming out of me. I couldn't fathom why I was being asked that question at that moment. I said, "Your job is to take care of this problem. I'm already a Mom." Before I was asked that, I should have been asked if I had any other children, followed by an empathetic statement like "I'm so sorry that this happened to you."

A second medical challenge arose in my forties when I went to the hospital for a bladder ultrasound. I take these tests fairly often to check on bladder function. In this instance my mom had given me a ride to the hospital. She joined me in the examination room to help me get on the examination table. I should point out that if hospitals and medical clinics had at least one examination table that could be raised or lowered to accommodate people with disabilities, we wouldn't always need to bring friends or family to help manhandle us onto tables that are placed at a height to accommodate staff, not patients with disabilities.

I was sitting on the table. Mom was in a chair in front of me. A nurse entered and put some paperwork on a small table, then turned to my mom and said "Is she sexually active?" Mom looked like she wanted the floor to swallow her up. She didn't answer the nurse's question.

I couldn't believe what I had heard. That nurse didn't know whether the woman with me was a neighbor, an attendant, a relative, a family member or another patient.

I said, "Never mind, we're leaving. And by the way, I have two children so you figure it out!" If that information was needed as part of the test, the nurse should have asked my mom to step out while personal questions were being asked. When I reached home I called the hospital's ombudsman to register a formal complaint, and I returned to the hospital on another day, to be served by a more sensitive health professional.

Other challenges in my life often become realities because I can rarely be spontaneous. Transportation used by people with disabilities requires pre-planning and lots of waiting. There are times when I feel like I must have been impatient at waiting in my previous life. That may be why I have had to do so much of it over fifty-seven years in my current life. When you live as a disabled person in an able-bodied world you always have to be prepared. It's never as simple as deciding, "*I want to.*"

But no matter how much you prepare, social situations and the people within those situations can derail your plans.

Two examples—and whether they happened to me is not the point. They've happened to countless numbers of people with disabilities:

You have a job interview. You've gone to great lengths to study the company that needs a worker. You've become a walking encyclopedia about its activities and its culture. A friend has helped you go through a couple of dummy practice interviews for this job. You've chosen your interview ensemble so you will look like a consummate professional. You've put together a handout to leave with the interview team and had it professionally printed. And because of uncertainties about when your assisted transportation service would get you to the meeting site, you arrived forty minutes early.

But within the first five minutes of the interview, when you're enthusiastically giving the interview team your introductory pitch about your capacities, the faces of the interview team tell you all you need to know. They aren't listening. All they hear is the squeak or whirr of your chair entering and leaving the room.

You don't get a second interview.

You're a young adult, eager to meet other young people, and you've been invited to a singles dance in the recreation room of your new apartment building. You buy a new dress, you have your hair done, and you buy a pair of earrings that are simply stunning. You shine!

You arrive stylishly late. You introduce yourself and you're met with smiles and greetings. You settle in, quiet for a while, then you decide to use the conversational skills you've been practicing. You strike up a conversation with a young man sitting near you on the rec room couch. He responds politely when you ask him questions about himself, but he doesn't ask you anything about your own life.

You'd love to dance. While you can't move your feet across the dance floor, but your upper body can dance as well as anybody else.

When the music starts your young man (who has been looking over your shoulder to see who else is in the room) politely takes his leave. He asks another young woman to dance. He doesn't return to continue the conversation you started with him.

No matter how much you shine, you don't get to dance.

These two little stories may seem a bit mawkish, but versions of them are repeated in the lives of people with disabilities throughout their lives, often sapping what self-confidence they've been able to build up, and leading some of us to withdraw or to develop a rage-fed bitterness we keep bottled up as much as we can.

Our friends propose well-meaning solutions to our dilemmas—*"Just look for work in agencies that serve people with disabilities, where you will be understood"*…. *"Just take the initiative and ask young men to dance with you."*

They are right of course. We could reduce the field of possible job prospects by 80%, or we could exert 80% more effort than able bodied people to build our social networks, and that's sometimes what we do. Sometimes we feel we have no other choice.

But it wears us down.

THAT WAS THEN AND THIS IS NOW

Laural a paramedic who also taught youngsters about her profession.

Emily makes herself available to help her hair stylist win a competition

For most of my life I could quite easily perform many physical activities, despite the limitations that CP places on me. In my twenties and thirties I thought nothing of sliding out of my chair to sit on the carpeted living room floor and practice yoga poses. I didn't experience chronic pain. By grabbing my wheelchair armrests I could pull myself back up in a standing position, pivot myself back into the chair. I would use the same strategy to sit on the kitchen floor and wipe it clean, although that wasn't very successful. The moment I was back in the chair and moving, the wheels dirtied up the floor again. Once I even managed to lift a heavy turkey out of the freezer for Christmas dinner, without falling as I stood up to grab the bird.

But I can't do these things anymore. Why? Spending most of my first twenty four years in a manual wheelchair is one factor, because it produced repetitive strain injuries that manifested themselves years later.

I got my first official tiny tot manual wheelchair when I was six years old and about to start grade one. My first electric wheelchair helped me travel quickly through Carleton University's underground tunnels to make it to my classes on time. Apart from speeding to classes, I didn't use the power chair. It was bulkier than my manual one and I couldn't drive it into the dormitory washroom I shared with my room mates because the bathroom doorway was too narrow. Since power chairs can't be folded up, using it exclusively would have removed my freedom to get into the cars of friends and family so we could go places together. But twenty-four years of self-wheeling laid the foundation for repetitive strain injury in my overworked arms, neck, and shoulders.

My arms have always been more than just my arms. They are additional support mechanisms for my legs. They give my body extra stability when I stand up or reposition myself. But my right shoulder is now plagued by osteoarthritis. When I raise or lower my right arm beyond shoulder level, I get an immediate painful reminder of the toll that the years have taken.

I've always had bladder challenges because I can rarely access and use a washroom as soon as I should. I don't even know if I exactly know when I should use a washroom, since I've always had to wait to access one that I can use.

If I find myself to be very tired in the evening now, when I want to transfer out of my wheelchair my legs will decide to get really shaky or they will root themselves to the floor so I can barely move them. Sometimes I have to take a few minutes to stop trying to do what I need to accomplish and remind myself that I know what I need to do and that I can still do it. Right now, I must continue to do everything that I physically can, while it's still possible to do so.

Since I'm the only person that lives in my body, I'm the only person who has the right to determine what to do when things change and when I need to use my body and my assistive devices differently. I also have the right to see things changing and decide not to do anything differently. Some people with disabilities welcome information and judicious advice from others, but none of us need to be harped at by others, or have our rights to choice overridden by people who don't live in our bodies. We have a right to try, to fail, to try again, to adapt as we see fit.

At the same time, I understand I can no longer take my physical independence for granted. One day I might not have that capacity.

Why am I telling you this?

First of all, I want you to know that except for moments when I deal with chronic shoulder and arm pain, these changes are not highly disturbing to me. My limitations occasionally irritate or discourage me, especially when I need to spend time re-thinking how to do what I've always done, how best to re-organize my life, how to become even more patient and to figure out how I can willingly and gracefully accept more help and new kinds of help from others. I'm the first to admit that these changes aren't easy, but they gradually become my new normal.

The Ontario Federation for Cerebral Palsy says that people with cerebral palsy use up to five times the energy that able-bodied people use when walking or moving about. The aging process for folks with CP puts enormous stress on our bodies, including every limb. CP is often described as being non-progressive: that's true for brain function, but we often lose physical capacities earlier and more quickly than most people. But that doesn't make us helpless: it makes us adapters earlier and more thoroughly. The good news: the life expectancy of a person with CP is comparable to that of other folks, so I don't plan to die soon.

While I'm adapting to my aging-based physical life changes, I still can't accept the fears that some ambulatory people feel compelled to share related to accidents, along with their assumptions that these accidents will inevitably become realities in my life.

I recently chatted with someone I knew well in the past. She asked how things were going and I mentioned that I was doing well except for new pain in my right shoulder. Her final comment was, "You know if you were my sister, I would feel more at ease if you just moved into a supportive housing apartment. That way, you could have more help from people and there would never need to be a fear of anything bad happening."

I swallowed my more uncharitable comments and replied, "If I was your sister and I did that, whose life would I be living—yours or mine? I expect nothing other than to live my authentic life."

A component of that authenticity is my right to take risks, although I make plans and take precautions to minimize risk. Like everyone else I could get hurt or die as a consequence of living my life, but if that were to be the final outcome of my life choices and a result of bearing witness to myself, then it is what it is.

I worked full-time for twenty-eight years in permanent government jobs before I was encouraged to take a two year contract position. Due to boredom and lack of opportunity for advancement in my preceding job, I happily accepted the contract offer in 2012. The contract ended two years later. I have never once regretted the contract choice I made.

At 52 I was no longer working. Six interviews, 607 job applications, and four years later I'm still not working, and in the spring of 2018 I stopped applying. I'm trying to see if I can once again tutor students. I did it successfully in the past: I love to see the light go on in someone's eyes when they finally understand a previously incomprehensible concept.

I would be lying if I didn't say that this has been the hardest "now" I have had to accept. I miss working because it put me on a level playing field with able-bodied people. My work ethic and collaborative leadership style matched or exceeded those of many others. Over the first two years of not working, I discovered that I wasn't eligible for government funding assistance because I have assets like my beautiful but modest townhouse. So I've enhanced my money management skills even more with the advice of an amazing financial advisor. By using minimal amounts of my retirement savings I've kept my house and fed myself, my daughter, and other important people who need to eat. That's good, but I miss being able to provide the small gifts and treats that I used to offer to people in need. My current life doesn't allow for financial splurges or vacations, other than whatever takes place in the back yard.

But this phase of my life has given me tangible rewards.

It has given me a longer and stronger connection with my younger daughter as she makes her way through her life and college.

It has allowed me to be strong, insightful, and supportive when helping close friends as they encounter life's challenges.

Since I was little, I've known I wanted to help people. I didn't always know how I would do it but I knew I wouldn't be happy unless my life was defined by service to others. But I sometimes help too much and I struggle to let people self-heal. I've learned that often you can tell people what you think is the answer, but until they figure it out themselves, it won't resonate. And just as I, a woman with a disability, am offended by people who want to help too much or too quickly, I mustn't create offense by over-helping others in my life.

I'm grateful for the difficulties I went through. I recognize that the most painful times in my life were the most deeply transformative. Without them, I wouldn't be who I am or where I am. They were necessary. They were transitory.

I am always working on myself. I am committed to self-growth and eager to find ways I can become more open-minded, more aware and more loving. My life goal is to know that I helped even just a few people, even just a little. I don't have to save the world. In fact, I don't really care to. I'm happy to help those within easy reach of my hands and heart.

I was blessed with the opportunity to raise two girls with beautiful souls. I'm now the proud mother of two young women who are finding their own ways to help people.

As a pre-teen and as a teenager Laural was an excellent gymnast and dancer. Even then I saw in her the determination to excel that characterizes her to this day. Laural has been a paramedic for four years now and she is attending university in Winnipeg to become a nurse. She is thinking about whether she will give up her medic job to become a full-time nurse or whether she will choose to do both jobs, each on a part-time basis. She is also thinking about joining the STARS Air Medical Crew. STARS (the Shock Trauma Air Rescue Society) is a Canadian non-profit helicopter air ambulance organization that provides emergency care and transportation for critically ill and injured patients.

Whatever choices Laural makes, she will remain committed to helping people in need. I couldn't do her job even if I had the physical capacity to do it. She feels an emotional bond with people in distress, while at the same remaining detached enough to apply her skills methodically to help them. As for me, I would tip the scales too often in the direction of emotion: I am easily tearful when I help someone, especially if I sense they are suffering or hurt.

Emily has her sister's drive to excel too. A graduate of a modelling school, she shows both poise and more than a touch of post-teen elegance. But since one can't eat elegance, her skills as a chef have been more than welcome in our family. Em has completed her studies in the Protection, Security and Investigation Program at Humber College in Toronto. She was one of only ten students invited to participate in a job shadowing program that taught her how to identify and prevent bank fraud. Em has been an honor student, very near the top of her class.

I'm proud that Em learned how to prevent or control fraud. Like her sister, she has a highly analytical dimension to her personality. She also has the soul of a helper, a quality she honed in high school when she helped a young boy with fetal alcohol spectrum disorder to do well academically and to learn how to function socially in a classroom setting. He developed his capacities with Emily's consistent, well thought-out help. In Em's mind and soul, protecting and nurturing are inseparable partners in making the world a better place.

WHAT I'VE LEARNED AND MESSAGES I WANT TO SHARE

I want to share what I've learned from spending my life using a wheelchair, what my parenting taught me and how that role has changed over time. I hope that what I say will encourage you to take a risk and to consciously live your life.

After deciding to have children and then being blessed with my two accomplished daughters, I knew (perhaps for the first time) that I alone should define what my own authentic life should look like and what steps I should take to live it. Before that revelation I had been compliant or I had merely reacted against others rather than charting my own positive course: I had lived trying to learn to get clear insights into what society expected of me so I would be accepted by everyone. I had either rebelled or pandered to what I thought the world expected of me. Neither way of acting gave me the outcome I wanted—a sense of living my life on my terms. Both ways of acting distracted me from defining my own values. Even my decision to abandon the effort to walk was, in retrospect, an act of rebellion unguided by a life vision.

The fact that most of my life has not been "traditional" shaped the values I developed. For example, since I don't walk, I knew I could never exert physical authority over the kids, so I embraced the values of provided opportunities for them to express their feelings and desires. I easily became comfortable taking more time than most parents do to explain to them why I thought they should or shouldn't do something. I negotiated with them.

Some folks around me assumed my approach would fail. They distrusted the ability of children to listen to reason and to negotiate with an adult. They feared my approach would produce undisciplined children who would run amok, ignoring adult advice and supervision, doing only what their whims dictated.

But that didn't happen. They became expert little negotiators, sensitive to the desires of others, willing to give and take.

My girls quickly notice human circumstances and think about how they can help anyone who faces a challenge. When Laural was about six years old, she and I went to the Toronto Art Gallery one summer with her godmother so that she and her godmother's son could take part in the AGO's kids' programs. We all had a great day. As we left the Gallery to return home, Laural saw a man sitting on the sidewalk. "Mom, that man looks hungry. Can I give him some money please?" For a moment my adult mind reverted to stereotypical thoughts about people living on the street: if I gave him money, he would likely use it to buy alcohol or drugs. But then I saw the deep look of concern on Laural's face and a ten dollar bill made it from my hand to hers. Joyfully she took it over to the man and she got a "Thank you, God bless you" and I got an ear-to-ear smile on my girl that lasted for a long time.

Like her sister, Emily also watches the world around her, alert to opportunities to help others.

Shortly after she started college, Em came home from school one day and said, "Mom, I was late for an afternoon class today."

"How come?" I said.

"I went across the street for lunch and when I was coming back I noticed a girl on the other side of the street in a manual wheelchair. She looked like a student I'd seen before at Humber. She was trying to wheel the chair over a big snowbank to get back to the college, but the chair kept sliding backwards. I yelled: 'Hi, are you a Humber student? Do you need help to get over here? I can give you a hand.' She nodded, so I ran across the street to her and I said, 'Hi, I'm Emily, My mom uses a wheelchair too, so I know how tough a snowbank can be.' The girl said, 'I tried to get back to school this way because I knew it would take a really long time to wheel all the way around the snowbank to get to the sidewalk, and I'm already really cold.' So I kicked down the snowbank she was trying to get over. Since I've also pushed you outside sometimes, Mom, I offered to push her back to the college on the slushy sidewalk so she wouldn't be late for her class and I could also make it to mine. It took longer than I expected because slush kept clogging the small front wheels, slowing us down. But I helped her back to school safely. My professor was annoyed because I was late for class, but I did the right thing."

I let myself feel very proud of her. She had acted on an immediate helping instinct. She does it all the time, quietly, with no fuss.

As my girls have gotten older my mothering role has changed. I think of myself now as a consultant, not a manager. As in the corporate world, good consultants offer expertize only when asked, couch it diplomatically, and expect that at least half of what they say will be ignored. Granted, I still sometimes fight the urge to impart whatever knowledge my years of living have given me, but now I preface my advice with phrases such as "One possible solution might be …" or "You're probably looking at many issues, but one thing to consider is …"

As a mother of young adult children I still strive to be respectful. It's common for even good parents to blurt out a well-intentioned, but oh-so-poorly-phrased criticism to an adult child: "You're not going to wear that, are you?" or "What kind of job is that?" If I thought a friend was making a big mistake I would talk to him carefully and tactfully. I am learning to exercise the same respect and compassion with my young adults. At the same time, grown children can hear implied criticism in just about everything a parent might say, so I try to save my advice for things that matter.

Despite my girls' entry into adulthood, I still find occasional opportunities to support and nurture their self-confidence and independence. I encourage my girls to take what they know and use it to their advantage. I'm quick to say," I'm sure you will figure out what will work best for you." I hope my girls have learned from me that there are many ways to achieve personal goals. You just need to start by being engaged in an activity in a way that makes sense to you, even if it doesn't make sense to anyone else. And even if the entire world tells you to do something, don't do it unless it makes moral and practical sense to you.

My wheelchair taught me that I'm the only one who knows and understands the body I live in and the mind that guides this body through the snares and opportunities the universe provides. Only I will know what will and will not work for me. While I learn from others, I can't always readily accept the suggestions of professionals and others who immediately or automatically assume they know what's best for me. Good people may have good intentions, and may have degrees that seem to validate their thoughts and actions, but they don't live with the realities that I do. For me their suggestions are only suggestions, not rules to be obeyed. Yet it's surprising how often experts are offended if I assert my right to decide.

I've learned that I'm stubborn to a fault. I'm also stubborn to a virtue.

I've learned not to buy into the fears that able-bodied people sometimes project on me—fears that lead them to want to wrap me in the cotton wool of their concern. When I chose to live my life by using a wheelchair, it didn't mean I would find myself in less daily danger than other people face. Like everyone, I've had to learn how to develop techniques that work for me.

As part of well-meant concern, some folks have suggested that I need a Life Line Medic Alert System in my house so I can call for help if I need it. Right now, my cellphone usually serves that function. I might change my mind about this, but in the past and even now, my instinct says that the system will provide a false sense of security, aimed at comforting the people who don't live with me or live my life. If I fall and hurt myself when I'm doing something that I consider to be part of my authentic life and I can't reach my cell phone, then I've taken a risk and paid the price. Yes, I've crashed my wheelchair on occasion and I've hit unexpected bumps that threw me out of the chair. But walking people slip on banana peels and walk into walls, so we're even.

Until we require mountain climbers, race car drivers, and all other risk-takers to attach those devices to themselves, a double standard is being imposed on me. The difference between me and a race car driver is that my risks will be way more familiar to the average person.

My wheelchair has taught me that I'm at my best when I'm trusted by others and when I'm helping someone who needs support. These opportunities are gifts that set my soul on fire.

Early in my life I sensed that most people saw me as a bundle of deficits, a messy collection of needs that could only be met through the kindly intervention of others. As a result, I look at every person I meet with an eye to determining the strength and goodness embedded in them. If they need help with learning, I collaborate with them to discover how learning will best work for them. I highlight their positive attributes and achievements no matter how small. If a person can't get the learning help they need from me, then I haven't yet ascertained how they learn.

I also know myself well enough to recognize that I learn about the lives of others through intense listening, coupled with reasonably good intuition. I ask questions when they need to be challenged, or when clarity and focus in thinking is necessary. I try to offer suggestions only when advice is sought—although, being far from perfect, I'm not always successful at it.

Dear Reader, if you have a disability or other challenge, please know that I'm not suggesting that you replicate any part of my life, unless one of my approaches or ideas speaks loudly to you. As you can imagine, living independently when it was expected I would live in an institution, or choosing to have children as a single mother with a disability, were not easy to achieve, but I was absolutely driven to do those things. I've never had regrets about these big directions in my life even though from time to time I've had regrets about some of the tactics I chose to get there. If others aren't driven to do such things, they shouldn't do them.

But I am a drop in a large ocean of insight. The wisdom of others often speaks to me.

Physicist Stephen Hawking spoke to me when he said that disabled people should concentrate on things their disability doesn't prevent them doing well, and don't regret the things it interferes with. He cautioned us not be disabled in spirit as well as physically.

Figure Skater Scott Hamilton spoke to me when he said that the only disability in life is a bad attitude.

Actress Anne Bancroft spoke to me when she said she got stubborn and dug in when people told her she couldn't do something when she thought she could. She believed it went back to her childhood when she had problems in school because of her learning disability.

Comedian, journalist and disability rights activist Stella Young spoke to me when she said that disability is often framed, in medical terms, as the ultimate disaster and certainly as a deficit.

FINAL WORDS FROM FRIENDS

When I started writing this book, I asked a few friends to say anything they wanted to say about disability or ability or the fate of the universe. I wasn't fishing for compliments, but more than a few kind words ended up on the end of my fishing line.

This is what four of my friends said (I hope they forgive me for my minor edits of their major contributions):

From my friend who rides a motorcycle far better than I can...

This is how I define authenticity: devoted to your true nature.

This is how to maintain authenticity: mindfulness.

This is my view of ability: that most able bodied people take their ability for granted, that it deteriorates, that there are varying levels of ability, that it requires maintenance. Many people don't know anyone who is disabled. I believe that a physical disability does not equal a mental or emotional one. To the contrary, I believe that folks with physical disabilities often develop keen skills in other areas and become incredibly resourceful when approaching challenges.

This is what I feel is society's perception of ability and disability: I think the perception is that people with a physical disability often have a mental disability ... or are treated as such. Perhaps society believes that people with disabilities are fully covered and cared for... or that they have someone close to help. I think society fails to see the daily struggles of those with disabilities... like how they manage personal details, food shopping, getting into bed, caring for children, banking, cleaning, and cooking.

How do I see this changing in future? I believe that the stereotype is changing via social media. Perhaps the able bodied are becoming kinder and more attentive to those around them. I see technology working in favor of people with disabilities, perhaps more specifically with amputees who haven't lost brave hearts who are now able to sky dive, bungee jump, climb, ride, and surf with the help of newly discovered aids and materials... not to mention the improvements made to simple day to day tasks. Transportation will become more accessible and more funding will be put towards research to trial to aid the disabled.

From my friend who has expanded the horizons of my spirit...

Humanity is gradually making progress towards consensus that the essence and value of a human being are independent of physical, intellectual and even mental properties..... As a teenager, after struggling for her entire young life to overcome physical disability, Lisa realized that the sacrifices she was making for her physical well-being were encroaching upon her intellectual, social, and personal development, at which point she made the decision to abandon the intense, unremitting, and arduous struggle to retain the ability to walk, and accept that for the sake of her education and personal development, to give up her ambulatory mobility. This is a decision of gravity, importance and difficulty that few of us will ever have to make.

Her courageous decision has been vindicated by all that she has accomplished since then. She has graduated from university, and has given birth to, and raised two beautiful, healthy daughters. She had successful careers with the March of Dimes, the Region of Peel, and Metrolinx. She has become a pathfinder and advocate for people who need help navigating the social services and health care systems. She has discovered and cultivated her talent for the written word. She is a life-long learner who actively studies to improve her skills in many areas, including spiritual development and the capacity to serve others.

From my friend who is wise in both official languages...

The Lisa Effect

My first real experiences with people who faced functional and/or mobility challenges occurred in the 1980s, when, as marketing manager for a transit system, I developed a travel training program for young adults. Truth be known, I didn't know what I was doing and it was difficult to find information on issues dealing with disabilities, especially as they related to travel. Nevertheless, the new program helped a number of people to use transit for daily commute to school or work. I learned much from my young customers and I was grateful for that.

Fast forward to the early 1990s: in a new home, I met most of my neighbors in person except for Margaret, who phoned to welcome me to the neighborhood and to ask if I had time for some volunteer work. She was coordinator for a charitable organization that helped people get back on their feet after a set-back, illness or tragedy. When I met Margaret in-person I realized that she herself would never get back on her feet; a medical accident in her 20s left her unable to move from the waist down. Now in her 70s, a loving wife and mother, an active volunteer, traveler, and party hostess, this vibrant woman proved that she didn't take life sitting down, wheelchair or not. She passed away in her 80s, but her spirit inspired me to prioritize transit accessibility for people with disabilities in Ontario.

And now, fast forward to the 2000s and to dear Lisa. I met her when she agreed to participate in a focus session to analyze whether proposed transit smartcard fare equipment and software could easily be accessed, understood, and used by everyone, including people with mobility challenges. While all participants were wonderfully helpful, Lisa stood out. If this had been a Facebook connection, she would have been an instant "like". We became business colleagues and we soon became friends. As I learn about her life-story I never cease to be in awe of her. I have a much better understanding of the endless challenges faced by people with disabilities, yet Lisa lets nothing stop her. Her creativity, problem solving skills, kindness, bottomless patience, and her drive to make things better for everyone, makes things better. It is the spirit of Lisa, and of others strong enough to push on as she does, that makes life better now and for the next generation of people with mobility and/or health challenges. Her enthusiasm is infectious, and we cannot help but to also want to make the world better, for all of us. And I dearly love her for it.

From my globe-trotting, world-loving friend...

This brave, honest woman's story will influence the lives of others with or without obvious disabilities.

This is a Warrior Woman. She challenges assumptions.

Our association was at first professional. I was startled when she wheeled into a committee meeting, a beautiful, dark haired young woman with a pregnant belly. I quickly learned how intelligent and competent she is. I marveled that with very few notes she could produce such concise, meticulous minutes of a meeting. Over the next few years of inter-organizational work she continued to impress. I realized we were becoming friends when I was invited to a baby shower for her second daughter. I then became more intimately aware of her life, its desires and challenges.

Lisa says it was easier being born into her body than to slowly or suddenly lose what one has. It is the life she was given and she is determined that it be a full, "normal", and productive life, which it surely is! She teaches by example and through advocacy for many others. She gives much more than she receives, in work and in friendship. Her friends feel cherished. She is love personified.

Through this friendship and my past work with people with MS, what do I think society now believes about people with dis-abilities? We have had our consciousness raised, in learning to value the humanity of all people, recognizing the value they bring to the fabric of our society. They are people with rich lives and deep loves, like everyone else.

Our society has increased its commitment to paying some of the costs of inclusion; the activities of independent daily living, employment, transportation, structural changes, and housing. Still, there is so much more we can do to assist with these challenges.

Too often I hear people in wheelchairs being talked down to, talked over or worse, ignored. We need to challenge our presumptions and assumptions. Lisa meets them head-on daily with grace and unreasonable patience. Read her story. You'll be amazed.

ABOUT THE AUTHOR

A graduate of Carleton University and the Sheridan College Human Services Management Program, Lisa Jones has worked extensively in the fields of support services and transit services for people with disabilities and community health planning. She has received the Pilot Club of Ontario's Disabled Professional Woman of the Year Award and the Judge George Thompson Award for service to people with disabilities in Ontario.

Lisa is the mother of two accomplished and personable daughters, and she is junior co-owner of a feisty cat named Meeko.

Lisa lives in Mississauga Ontario. She can be reached at lisadj@rogers.com.

Printed in Canada